The Fierce Beauty Club

About the Author

ELIZABETH HERRON, M.A. is an educator and consultant with more than 20 years' experience teaching women's psychology and male-female communications. Currently, she is the executive director of the Gender Relations Institute and the Fatherhood Coalition. She works as a psychology instructor at Santa Barbara City College, the Santa Barbara County Jail, and Pacifica Graduate Institute.

Elizabeth is the author of numerous articles and book chapters and is the coauthor of *What Women and Men Really Want: Creating Deeper Love and Understanding in Our Relationships*. She has appeared as an expert on gender issues on numerous national television and radio shows, and has written for metropolitan newspapers on this topic. She maintains a private consulting practice that specializes in guiding women toward developing a deeper connection with their innate power and beauty. She is also the proud mother of two wonderful young women.

To contact the author, please visit www.fiercebeauty.com or write to:

P.O. Box 4782
Santa Barbara, CA 93140

The
Fierce Beauty
Club

Girlfriends Discovering Power and
Celebrating Body and Soul

Elizabeth Herron

ELEMENT

Boston, Massachusetts • Shaftesbury, Dorset
Melbourne, Victoria

Text © Elizabeth Herron 2000
© Element Books, Inc. 2000

Published in the USA in 2000 by
Element Books, Inc.
160 North Washington Street
Boston, MA 02114

Published in Great Britain in 2000 by
Element Books Limited
Shaftesbury, Dorset SP7 8BP

Published in Australia in 2000 by
Element Books Limited for
Penguin Australia Limited
487 Maroondah Highway, Ringwood, Victoria 3134

Library of Congress Cataloging-in-Publication Data available.

ISBN 1-86204-787-1

Printed and bound in the United States by Courier

Contents

For my fierce and beautiful daughters,
Tashina and Noelani—
May your spirits shine and your dreams
come true.

Acknowledgments

MY DEEPEST GRATITUDE goes to my husband, Aaron Kipnis, for his unflagging confidence in me—believing in my work when I had lost faith and encouraging me to hold steadfastly to my deepest dreams. I want to thank Caroline Pincus for her elegant, enthusiastic and graceful style of bringing clarity and focus to my writing, and my agent, Tom Grady, for his persistence and unfailing good humor.

Many wonderful, juicy, strong women inspired this work, providing me with warm hearts, insight and generosity of spirit. To the original Fierce Beauties, my dear friends Helen, Dona, Patty, Francie White, my sisters Tory, Damaris and Johanna, Las Chicas Locas and the many other women who have been an essential part of this wild ride into the feminine soul—I wish you thirteen thank yous and honey in the heart.

Introduction

MY WORLD fell apart when I was 12 years old. The year after John F. Kennedy's sudden death broke the heart of the nation, my mother's death broke the heart of our family. Struggling with alcoholism and severe depression for years, she finally took her own life within days of her 40th birthday. She left a husband and four daughters in her disturbed wake. Like many women of her generation, who came of age in the late '40s and early '50s, she completely lost her way. As a result, I found myself negotiating the pitfalls of adolescence without mothering or the guidance and support of another female relative or mentor.

Forced into an early adulthood, I coped as well as I could, mostly through finding various men to fill the gaping holes in my heart. By the time I was 20 years old, I had had a number of failed relationships, and had pitifully low self-esteem, anxiety attacks, depression, insomnia, frequent nightmares and poor health. I also had a small daughter of my own. Out of sheer desperation and following some deep homing instinct like a carrier pigeon, I began to seek out the feminine energy that was missing from my life.

Over the next 15 years I participated in various types of women's groups, retreats and classes. I made forays into history, religion, psychology, mythology and anthropology, looking for information about female heroines and spiritual leaders.

And I began to make deep, abiding friendships with other women struggling with the same kinds of issues. In the past, I had had few close relationships with women, regarding them as competitors for the male attention I craved. But these new friendships became a current of fresh life that flowed into my veins, invigorating, strengthening and revitalizing my being.

Catalyzed by my own personal quest, my passion for women's psychology moved me into a professional career that focused primarily on women's transformation and gender issues. In this work as an educator, seminar leader and corporate consultant over the past 20 years, I have observed that many contemporary women, even the most highly successful ones, are experiencing a crisis in their self-esteem, as well as in their capacity for self-care. There is a growing sense that many of us have lost the ground underneath us, contributing to a diminishing of women's spirit and vitality.

Under the weight of rapidly changing role expectations and the ever-increasing demands of work and relationships, the fabric of many women's personal identity has become tattered and torn. Older women drink more alcohol, smoke more cigarettes, have higher rates of divorce, heart disease and hypertension, and increasingly report feeling isolated and alone. Younger women fall prey to rampant eating disorders, as well as unprotected and uncommitted sexual relationships. More children than ever before live in poverty. Our daughters do not necessarily inherit a better world.

This may surprise those of us who came of age during the last 30 years. To varying degrees, we became "liberated women." We had big dreams, attempting to leave behind the legacy of the generations of women who came before us. We were determined not to be like our mothers—financially and emotionally dependent on men, bound to the needs of children, and without the freedom of choice to control our own destinies. We aspired to autonomy—desiring successful careers, financial self-sufficiency, and emotional and sexual freedom.

The downside of these social changes, however, is a growing confusion about what it means to be a woman. We have rejected many of the values of traditional femininity but collectively have failed to create new social and spiritual guidelines that practically and effectively assist women as they move through their life cycles. Generation X spokeswoman Katie Roiphe laments this absence of meaningful structure in *Last Night in Paradise* saying, "We are caught in the paradoxes of our own excesses. We live with both the sexual revolution and the reaction against the sexual revolution."

No one could deny that women have made tremendous progress in many arenas. Companies owned by women now employ more people than the Fortune 500 combined. The wage gap is narrowing, and our net worth is growing. Women are now the majority of managers and university students filling the pipelines to higher ranks of achievement.

While there are widespread indications that women may have increased their opportunities in the world, however, in many cases their inner lives are still in disarray. We have taken the first collective steps toward *external* freedom. Now, our next challenge is to create an *internal* state of emotional, psychological and spiritual freedom that matches the pace of our social, economic and political gains.

In *The Lipstick Proviso,* author Karen Lehrman asserts that following the first two great waves of feminism, which focused on political and economic freedoms, "the next wave [of feminism] needs to be primarily devoted to developing our emotional independence . . . now that the cages of constrictive femininity have finally been opened, women, in many ways, have to be remade." The purpose of this book is to provide women with the tools they need for access to a more sustainable, healthy and rewarding power that can free us from the internal psychological cages that limit us.

This book heralds a third stage of women's journey toward genuine freedom. The forefront of women's healing today is the need to determine our own definition of power, one that is rooted in an awareness of the fundamental developmental needs of women as we move through our lives. In my groups, I hear women repeatedly express a yearning for a new understanding of power that can help us move through life without splitting off our minds from our bodies, our intellects from our hearts, our work from our families and our self-image from our souls.

We can discover this power through a deep connection with the essence of femininity—what one could call the feminine soul. This natural source of healthy femininity, which bubbles up inexorably from the depth of women's psyches, informs us about our deepest needs for creative and emotional expression. It is a source of true essential beauty for women and is an antidote for the tyranny of external beauty to which so many women in this culture feel subjected.

When connection with this deep part of them is intact, women report an intrinsic sense of value and strength that continues to deepen and evolve as they become older. The power that springs from the feminine soul moves beyond superficial notions of beauty that create those "I'm not pretty enough" despots in the female psyche. It is instead a potent knowing that being female is a unique, dynamic, passionate and multi-faceted experience. The flame of women's will to power, achieved through the vehicle of a female body, burns brightest and longest when it comes from a connection with the feminine soul. It is the desire that each one of us has to be alive, to thrive and to live to the fullness of our female potential.

Discovering and sustaining a connection with the feminine soul is best done in the company of other women. *The Fierce Beauty Club* tells the story of a group of eight women, including myself, who regularly met together for several years in an art studio in the foothills of Santa Barbara, California. Frustrated with the dearth of information available to women that did something more than endlessly describe our victimization, we looked for concrete positive solutions to our problems. We were neither feminists nor traditionalists in orientation, but thought of ourselves as what Alice Walker aptly named "womanists." We celebrated our femininity as well as our independence, and found the company of other women a source of inspiration and support.

The Fierce Beauty Club recounts the stories of the members of the group, who became the goddesses of their own worlds— dancing, creating, loving and crying, claiming the power and sacredness of their being. We learned how to "mother" each other, and through seeing our true worth reflected in the mirror of loving female faces, we gave birth to ourselves. In the time we spent together, we rediscovered the joy of being female. We shared information and experiences that helped us to learn how to be women and to understand the unique gifts we had to give to the world.

In this particular group, my role was as a leader who facilitated and focused our time together. Over the years, however, I have also been a participant in similar groups countless times. Through both these experiences I have come to deeply value the ways that women can help each other. It is very difficult to make changes in our lives without ongoing positive feedback and encouragement from others. I am writing this book to offer an opportunity for a wider circle of women to benefit from the valuable experiences we shared and to encourage others to create "girlfriend groups" as vehicles for this process.

The information in this book can be accessed in a number of ways. I recommend that women seek out other like-minded women and form a Fierce Beauty group. This can be done either with a formal leader or without one. You do not need to be in a group, however, to get benefit from this material. Individuals can effectively use much of the information and exercises on their own. Certainly, women's groups are not everyone's cup of tea. It can also be fun to explore this material with a friend. I go out to dinner a couple times a month with a close girlfriend, and we help each other remember who we are and where we're going. Quality time with one woman can be every bit as valuable as time spent in a group.

The nine-step program described in this book is designed to help women love and believe in themselves. It aims to teach women how to embrace *both* their femininity and their power without feeling that one or the other must be sacrificed. I also want women to learn how to tend their own needs while also staying in connection with others. So often, we either live for ourselves or we live for others. We vacillate between selflessness and selfishness, independence and codependence. This book suggests that women can achieve "inter-dependence" with their loved ones. We can acknowledge the truth of our profound desire for intimacy and companionship, while also fiercely protecting our needs for autonomy and personal expression.

I have come to believe that the greatest strength women have comes from knowing what our gift to the world is and how to go about giving it. This becomes the organizing center and the telos, or the end result, of our experience. We have only just begun to bring forth all the potential creativity that lies within us. My prayer for this book is that it be sustenance for the seeds that lie waiting to sprout within our feminine souls. May it be the sunlight, the gentle spring rain and the rich earth needed for new growth and rich harvests.

CHAPTER 1

Welcome to the Fierce Beauty Club

*Apart, we were small, separate;
together we were the best of each of us,
a whole shimmering world.*
—Geneen Roth

THE FIERCE BEAUTY CLUB began a few years ago when a group of women assembled in a converted garage. Eight of us arrived, faces alight with expectation and trepidation, ready to take a collective leap into the unknown. Sophie, an artist friend of mine, was kind enough to offer the use of her studio, poised delicately but firmly on the side of a low rolling hill overlooking the California coastline. Outside, we were surrounded by hills covered by bright yellow mustard grass and purple lupine.

Inside, painted canvases surrounded us with wild, colorful images of women (her favorite subject), creating an evocative ambiance for the journey we were beginning. There was a slightly worn oriental rug on the floor, a pot-bellied iron stove that looked like a relic of another age and a variety of tatty but comfy old couches and easy chairs. The evocative scents of turpentine, wood smoke and sandalwood incense permeated the air. One corner of the room was cluttered with painting supplies, easels and stacks of canvases. Another corner had a desk with a computer and a printer. Next to it stood a gray metal filing cabinet and a bookshelf filled with computer manuals, accounting and tax books.

The women had responded to my invitation to participate in a women's group that would explore feminine identity, self-esteem and creativity. They ranged in age from 22 to 71 and came from a variety of backgrounds. Sophie, her wild auburn hair framing her round face like a halo, welcomed us as she poured hot tea for us in lovely porcelain cups. "This is my granny's tea set," she said affectionately. "It's the only thing I have of hers and it seemed appropriate to use it tonight. She loved to have tea parties with her lady friends." As we sipped tea and munched cookies, we introduced ourselves and shared some of the issues that drew us to the group.

Jenny, a 45-year-old wearing a muted green oversized sweater and baggy slacks, had shoulder-length gray hair. It was parted in the middle and fell like curtains on either side of her oval face. She said, twisting her hands together nervously, "I am very confused about my life right now. I have two teenagers and one kid in college. They're all so involved in their own lives that they hardly seem to notice my existence anymore.

"I'm one of the few women that I know today who actually did the traditional wife and mother thing. I chose to stay home with my kids, and I was always proud of making that decision. After 25 years, I'm still married to my husband, which is practically unheard of these days. But it's been a long time since I felt close to my Sam. He's very engaged in his work as a claims adjuster at an insurance company. I guess I'm pretty depressed. I go through my days not really knowing what to do with myself."

Alex, a blond, athletic-looking 29-year-old wearing a purple velour jogging outfit, responded, "I guess I envy your free time. I'm going nuts trying to take care of my two kids and get my business off the ground. My kids are still small and they constantly need me. Dylan is five and Katie is three and a half.

"I work as a freelance sales rep for local crafts people. Business is starting to pick up, which is really exciting. It's what I've been wanting for a long time. But I'm not handling any of it very well. I worry a lot, have trouble sleeping at night, and end up yelling at my kids more than I should. Danny, my husband, is getting pretty fed up with how unavailable I am all the time. And we fight a lot. I feel stretched to the max. It was hard to make time to come to this group, but I know I need to do something for myself."

Lena, a feisty, zaftig, petite Latina woman in her late 50s, worked as a manager at a local bed and breakfast hotel. She had lovely long black hair that she wore twisted up on top of her head, held in place with a turquoise and silver comb. She said wistfully, "You guys are lucky to have husbands to complain about, I come home at the end of the day to an empty apartment. My son is grown up and lives on the East coast. I've been going through changes about being over 50 and single. Sometimes I think I'm going to end up one of those lonely old ladies that get abandoned in a state-run convalescent home. So I want you all to know," she joked, her dark eyes flashing, "I'm actively looking for a handsome Latin lover to take me salsa dancing."

"That sounds good to me," said Sophie, cupping her hands around her tea cup as the steam rose off the top. "Well, I just had my 40th birthday last month and nothing feels quite the same to me. For years I've run a successful accounting business out of this studio. I've always painted, but lately that's *all* I want to do. I'd like to sell my business and just paint for a while, but the very thought terrifies me. Michael, my husband, has been encouraging me to take the leap. He really believes in me, sometimes more than I do myself."

Sitting next to Sophie was an old friend of mine named Elinor, whom I had asked to join our group. Elinor was a 71-year-old retired nurse. "I think I'm the old lady in the group," she said, with a slight southern accent and a warm smile. "I've been a lot of different things myself over the years and times have sure changed since I grew up. The one thing I've learned is that whatever is going on now, it's gonna change soon. My husband died a year ago. We'd been married for 40 years." She paused as her eyes filled up with tears.

"As you can see, I haven't gotten over his death. I miss him terribly. Liz suggested I come to this group for the company and the support. But life goes on. I'm teaching several yoga classes. I have grandchildren that live nearby that are the joy of my life. Right now I feel more hopeful, like I'm on the edge of something new."

Allison was a pretty young woman in her early 20s, dressed in tight designer jeans and a tee-shirt. "I'm not used to talking in groups," she said diffidently, "but here goes. I just got married this last year to my high-school sweetheart and we'd like to have a baby at some point. I work as an office assistant and I've been going to the community college. My therapist suggested that it would be good for me to be in a women's group, but I'm kind of leery of the whole thing." She paused a little breathlessly and looked around at the other women. "You're all older than me and I feel intimidated by you."

Sylvia, a tall, big-boned 33-year-old dressed in a tailored pinstripe suit with short dark hair, who was sitting next to her patted her hand, "You're not the only one, this is scarier than hell. I'm a computer engineer and I spend most of my time at work where it's almost all guys. This is a whole new ball game for me.

"Even outside of work I've actually had more guy friends than women friends over the years. I've always felt sort of big and clunky and out of place around women. My life has been more about pursuing a career than looking for a husband. When I was studying in college, most of my friends spent a lot of time partying. Now I work long hours and I make good money. But I've noticed lately that I feel kind of empty. I don't have much intimate connection. Most of my relationships with men have been short-lived. But, so far, I'm enjoying being with all of you tonight," she said looking expectantly at the group. "I've been wanting to spend more time with women."

"I second that," I said, picking cookie crumbs out of my lap. "One of the reasons that I called this group together is that I think we all need regular doses of girlfriend time. Lately, I spend a lot of time alone in my room writing on my computer, or hanging out with my husband, Aaron. He's great, but I miss having more time to be with women. It's like not taking enough of an important vitamin."

As I reflected on our opening remarks, I realized that many of us had been away too long from an ongoing connection with other women and were feeling the ill effects of being uprooted from the rich earth of our female gardens. Women are relational beings. We do not thrive in isolation, particularly from other women. It is helpful to stay in touch with other like-minded women friends as we move through a world in which femininity and female roles are in tremendous flux.

Reawakening the Feminine Soul

Recently, in most of the gatherings I've been to with women, whether it's an informal lunch, a dance class, a baby shower or a class I'm teaching, I hear my friends and students express their hunger to spend more time with other women. And when this kind of quality time comes their way, their enthusiastic appreciation knows no bounds. Why this strong desire for girlfriend time? Why does it seem so important to us?

Over many years of working with women I've discovered that something quite wonderful and mysterious happens when groups of women come together to support and learn from one another. The group energy creates a metaphorical bowl or container in which the deep essence of our feminine nature, the feminine soul, is held and can then be experienced by those present. Reconnecting with the feminine soul helps women to remember who they are in a world that is often confusing and damaging to women's psyches.

The feminine soul is an intrinsic part of all women, a mysterious wellspring of inspiration, intuition, vitality, power and creativity that informs our identity as women. It is not bound by culture or history, but has its roots in what Carl Jung called the collective unconscious. We could think of the feminine soul as being the collective memory of women throughout time, a vast repository of our experience as women, as well as the seeds of our undiscovered possibilities.

Many women tell me that they feel disenfranchised, to some degree, from this source of strength and vision. Contemporary women are far more isolated than our forebearers. We partner and bear children in small, disconnected, discrete units. We are often removed either geographically or emotionally from our kinship systems, including our own mothers. Many of us work long hours and have little time for social connection and community-building activities. As a consequence, we may live without regular access to female community and a shared, tangible experience of the feminine soul.

In another time or place, we would have lived in intact multi-generational families, with mothers, grandmothers, aunties and sisters nearby. The work of our daily lives would often have been shared, including the rearing of children. Our female identities would, in these kinds of environments, have been cradled, mirrored and informed by a myriad of sources of femininity. If we needed guidance, it would have been there. If we needed help at any level, it would have been available. If we needed to know who we were, we would have had only to look around us.

Scientists studying the behavior of primates have discovered that collaborative groups of females can be essential for the survival of the species. Anthropologist Helen Fisher, in *The First Sex: The Natural Talents of Women and How They Are Changing the World*, explored the world of the female Bonobo chimps that create "friendship networks," consisting of older and younger females. The older females assist the younger female chimps with food collection and social support. Female chimps in these networks have more social status and successfully bear more young. In our culture we often lack the benefits of these cooperative kinship systems of women.

Because of this disruption in the fabric of female community, many of us have lost the compass or reference point that an ongoing connection with other close women can provide. This often produces a loss of self-confidence, inner strength, physical vitality, and a pervasive sense of insecurity. The pressures of modern life create expectations from many directions that women should be all things to all people. We are supposed to be superwomen, yet most women have fewer familial and social resources than ever. As a result, we are like cars limping along with missing cylinders or, worse, running on empty.

☀Fierce Beauty Tip

Reach out to a girlfriend you may not have seen for a while. Make a date to go out for dinner or lunch. Have fun and get down together. Take turns sharing some of the intimate details of your lives. Listen with an open heart, speak with a soft tongue and make a plan to get together regularly.

Rediscovering Our Female Cultural Roots

In addition to the work I've done with women over the years, I have also codirected the Gender Relations Institute with my husband, Aaron Kipnis. Our mission was to build bridges between women and men, using a council/dialogue process called Gender Diplomacy. We discovered, through hosting dialogues with thousands of people, that, in many ways, women and men inhabit different cultures. Much of the conflict between the sexes is the result of a clash between these two cultures with their very different values, protocols, behaviors and priorities. We discovered that one key to resolving many of the deep and painful issues that plague our individual identities, as well as our relationships, is to embrace one's own gender culture.

The movement toward multiculturalism in our country encourages ethnic groups to rekindle their nationalist spirit through exploring their cultural roots. Becoming aware of and celebrating one's unique culture enhances self-confidence and self-esteem. This is also true for women and men. We may be members of different cultures, but we don't necessarily know a great deal about our own culture, and we may not have spent much time with other members. For women, female culture is the garden in which the seeds of female power and health grow. It is the primary matrix in which we learn how to be women.

So when women come together without men, many of us feel like we've come home. Without even knowing why, we relax, "let down our hair," kick back and get down with the girls. We may not even realize the extent to which we may have been holding in, holding back, holding out and changing ourselves in subtle ways through being in the presence of men and male culture.

As we chatted for a while about the value of women's community, I noticed that Allison had a puzzled frown. "What do you think about all this?" I asked her, holding out my teacup for Sophie as she passed by with the pot.

"It sounds like you're becoming a separatist or something," she objected. "I'm not into that at all."

"Me either, I'm sick of all this male bashing that goes on," agreed Lena.

"I'm not an advocate of separatism," I responded, "and I definitely don't feel superior to men. But we can celebrate who we are without doing it at the expense of men. I don't think that's what we're about here at all. I do know, though, that we have lost a lot of our ground as women, and we need to find it again."

Female culture is a collection of behaviors, attitudes and social arrangements that is influenced by many sources. First, women share biological realities that affect the formation of our individual identities as well as our culture, as a whole. Our biological life cycle, from first menstruation, to child bearing, to menopause, is a string that links each individual pearl of a woman. And while biology is not the all of who we are, it is an indomitable taskmistress who roots us inextricably in the rawness of nature's cycles of growth. Evolutionary biology is discovering the extent to which the animal body may still reign supreme, dictating sexual and social choices through deeply coded genetic wiring. The fact that we have vaginas, can have babies and bleed monthly for a large part of our lives makes us profoundly different from men, despite any political agenda to the contrary.

Second, layered on top of the biological fundament are social structures that women have created throughout time to support our biological movements. These social structures guide us through the different developmental phases of life, teaching us the "how" of being a woman with specific roles and responsibilities to her family and community. Third, layered on top of the social construction of gender are our religious traditions, which provide the templates for gender roles, informing us through image and word what is acceptable or unacceptable behavior. Lastly, postmodern revisions of traditional gender roles have introduced a new set of considerations about the construction of femininity. Female culture is a broad river fed by these smaller tributaries.

Women on the Move

Women's culture has undergone transformation throughout history, as Elinor has witnessed during her long life. Currently, we live in the middle of perhaps the most drastic revolution in female culture to date. One of the primary catalysts for that change is women's capacity to control our ability to procreate at will. We are no entirely longer at the mercy of the enormous procreative force of nature whose only mandate is to produce more human life in service of the survival of the species. We can choose to give birth or not, according to our circumstances and individual desires. In 1800, the average woman gave birth to seven children. Currently, the average woman gives birth to just over two. Many women choose not to have children at all, a choice that would have been considered heretical not long ago.

This drawing of the line in the sand with Mother Nature has had profound effects on female culture. We now have a multitude of choices about the course of our lives. We can pursue multiple career paths and forms of creativity. Female gender roles are more varied and less rigidly defined. Our relationship to sexuality is liberated from the inevitable equation of sex equals pregnancy, and we are freer than ever before to explore sexual pleasure and expression for its own sake.

In addition, women's life expectancy has increased from 47.5 years in 1900 to 77 in 1999. There are growing numbers of postmenopausal women who are pursuing active lives and looking for an understanding of what life beyond 50 is all about. Some aspects of female culture, therefore, are in tremendous flux, being formed and reformed under the influence of changing biological and social realities. These now exist simultaneously with female cultural artifacts that have been with us since the beginning of time.

The upshot, however, of all this cultural flux is that many women receive, as they grow up, a confused and sometimes chaotic blend of traditional cultural values mixed with nontraditional, postmodern gender models. Many of us, as adults, experience this as an internal war between paradoxically different parts of ourselves struggling for expression. We are often a mix of old needs and modern feminist doctrinaire—a sort of Gone With the Wind meets The Second Sex. This muddy blend can leave us feeling inadequate, not only in the eyes of others, but most importantly, in our own!

We discussed this concept of female culture in our newly

formed group. Various women agreed that they could relate to the feeling of having lost their bearings.

"So Liz, you're saying we're confused about who we are?" asked Allison.

"Well, what do you think? Has that been true for you?" I replied.

"My mother is kind of a feminist. She's always wanted me to get a career together, and was pretty pissed when I got married to Billy last year," she answered thoughtfully, twisting a strand of her long blond hair around her finger. "I felt really torn between pleasing her and doing what I truly felt like I wanted to do. I guess that was all pretty confusing."

"I'm the complete opposite," laughed Lena. "My mother has never forgiven me for getting divorced and never producing any more grandbabies for her to dote on. You would think one would have been enough to make her happy."

"I'm trying to do both at the moment," said Alex. "I have small children *and* a career. Nobody else in my family did it like this. I often wish I had a better instruction manual that could tell me how to manage it all."

"I just feel lost," volunteered Jenny. "I got misplaced somewhere between diapers, the PTA and business dinners for my husband's company. I thought I was the ultimate mother and housewife. I was the one who took care of everyone else's children while they went to work. But now I don't have a clue what it means to be a woman."

The female psyche today is host to innumerable paradoxes. We aspire to independence but secretly yearn to be cared for and protected by a man. We aspire to sexual freedom but mourn the loss of genuine love and commitment in our relationships. As many studies have demonstrated, the most fulfilled women have it all—marriage, children and career, but the strain of sustaining such complex lives is driving us nuts.

The current state of female culture is like the land surrounding a volcano that has exploded. The streams of lava have drastically changed the landscape—redirecting hills, valleys, and rivers and even creating new virginal land. Beneath and around the new terrain are vestiges of the original landscape. There is tremendous new growth happening through the vehicle of the volcanic process, and the ancient land beneath supports that growth.

When we come together and examine who we are as women, it is as if we are pioneers together in this rejuvenated landscape, exploring and mapping the unknown, raw, freshly birthed feminine. We can give form and definition to the new parts of female culture while still standing on the ground and celebrating the richness of what came before. The new and the old work in tandem as a cocreating partnership, resulting in the dynamic mix that is the essence of female culture.

Fierce Beauty Tip

Create a Fierce Beauty journal to chronicle your personal explorations. At any given moment something inside us is being born and something is passing away. What is being born in you right now? In your journal write an invitation welcoming her into the world. Make a list of the resources that this new, fledgling aspect of your psyche will need in order to thrive.

Healing Female Shame

Feminist philosophy has helped bring about an awareness of gender stereotypes and the prison of traditional roles, but has, unfortunately, also rejected some aspects of female culture. At the core of feminism was a profound distrust of womanhood, as if women betrayed themselves just by virtue of being female. Many leaders of the women's movement expressed the fear that if one explored or even identified with "female culture," or femininity, then she was at risk for returning to the constricted roles of the '50s homemaker and wife—"the feminine mystique," as Betty Friedan named it. Freedom would arrive with the eradication of much of what we think of as being feminine.

As a result, one of the critical deficiencies of feminism was its collective failure to deal with the core of female oppression—women's innate distrust and dislike of themselves. One of the common themes that I hear over and over again when women tell their stories is the experience of feeling ashamed simply for being women. Feminism has identified men and the "patriarchy" as the source of this negativity. It is certainly true that some men, out of their own sense of inadequacy, fear women and need to diminish them. But we rob ourselves of the opportunity to heal this wound if we ignore our own responsibility for self-devaluing.

Gender shame takes many forms. We feel inadequate in our physical beauty. We feel ashamed that we have needs for connection and intimacy in our relationships. We feel that we are either too sexual or missing adequate interest. We either work too much at our careers and are insufficient parents and wives, or we don't work enough and are dependent on the men in our lives. If we are exclusively devoted to our children, we feel like our mothering is flawed. At work, our emotionality is unacceptable. At home, our needs for aloneness are unacceptable.

In so many arenas, our femininity seems insufficient, out of place, demeaned, unappreciated and even pathological. There are some indications that the average woman today is more unhappy and depleted than ever before. Danielle Crittenden writes in her recent book, *What Our Mothers Didn't Tell Us: Why Happiness Eludes the Modern Woman*, "The situation women wake up in today is more dire than the one of thirty years ago." She goes on to suggest that the root of the problem is that "we are cut off from those aspects of life that are distinctly and uniquely female."

In girlfriend groups, such as the one we were forming, we can heal female shame through affirming one another's value and replacing the negative messages with more useful and positive feedback. Any time we connect in positive ways with women, we can love and celebrate our femaleness. It is difficult for women to change these kinds of internalized programs without the help of regular, ongoing support. I brought the Fierce Beauty Club together so that we could help each other rewrite the script of our lives, providing new lines, new scenes and different, more interesting and fulfilling dramatic content.

Connecting Not Competing

One of the biggest obstacles to women bonding with one another is the pervasiveness of female competition. "Most of my friends think that me going to this group is really weird," related Allison. "We all feel very competitive with each other, even me and my best girlfriends. We don't want anybody to be too cute, or too cool."

"It's like that for me at work," said Sylvia. "The competition between the women there is deadly. I've started to distrust most of the women I work with. I've had some bad experiences where I confided in a female coworker about some problems I was having on the job and she used that information to try and undermine my job standing. She had her eye on my position. It was horrible."

Some of the women I've come in contact with through my work tell me that they have never had a positive experience of female friendship in their entire lives. They feel more betrayed by women than by men, and are more willing to trust men than women. Others may have had a close woman friend or two along the way, but, for the most part, feel alienated from other women. This is a tragic state of affairs because it robs women of such an enormous resource available to them—the comfort and insight of other women's shared experience.

Competition between women is a symptom of our alienation from our own power and beauty. Because these two qualities have become scarce commodities in female culture, competition between us is more deadly than ever. Older women often feel intense envy, even hatred, for younger women. Younger women feel judged and disliked by older women. Working women compete, as never before, for hard-to-win economic gains. The feminist concept of "sisterhood" seems elusive to many women.

There is also an unspoken agreement that women will betray a basic code of female culture if they break out of the familiar place of insufficiency and feel good about themselves. Geneen Roth calls this a "conspiracy of hunger...based on a belief that who I am is not enough, that in the cafeteria of life, I will never have a big enough tray." In Australia, they call it the "Tall Poppy Syndrome." Various teachers visiting there note that it is frowned upon to be different or exceptional in any way—to rise above the norm. Women are also encouraged by other women not to be tall poppies but to stay small and refuse distinction.

I recently had lunch with a friend of mine who had been ill and unable to keep up with her rigorous exercise workout. She was lamenting that she could only take walks and could not continue moving toward her goal of having a hard body. I told her that I aspired to softness not hardness. She was completely dumfounded at my response. I was breaking the code of "thinness rules!" for women. I had also broken the commandment that says "that shall not accept your body as it is."

These subtle but powerful aspects of female culture teach and maintain many destructive ideas about power and beauty. But when women come together for the purposes of rebuilding, recreating and reawakening themselves, we can enter into new social contracts with one another. We can establish new cultural protocols that encourage women to celebrate who they are, confer power and strength, and illuminate one another's true soul beauty.

In Search of the Lost Motherline

As we shared our stories during our first meeting, it became apparent that most of us lacked healthy, positive role models of women who were deeply and effectively rooted in their fierce femininity. Most of our role models were either dependent (often miserable) wives stuck in traditional roles, *femme fatale*–type women who used their sexuality to manipulate men, or feminist women, who often rejected their femininity altogether. We were missing role models of women who embraced their femininity, asserted responsibly their independence and individuality, and enjoyed and loved their female bodies as they were created by nature.

Ideally, older women, particularly our mothers and other female relatives, would transmit this positive feminine identity to younger women. And if it was not provided through the vehicle of family lines, our spiritual traditions should provide guidance for women to discover this part of their psyche. Unfortunately, the loss of value and respect for female culture in so many parts of our society has disrupted the natural process of initiation into the power and true beauty of the feminine soul.

Jungian analyst Naomi Lowinsky calls the inherited body of female wisdom that would traditionally be transmitted through our mothers and their grandmothers before them "the Motherline." This organic intuitive knowing, existing since the beginning of time, teaches women how to be women. The Motherline *is* the instruction manual that we always joke about wishing we had. It provides the social, moral and spiritual framework needed for the feminine soul to thrive. In our times, however, we have rejected so much of the traditional feminine paradigm that, in many ways, we've rejected the Motherline.

Our world is so different, our domains of endeavor so much

more complex, how could our mothers and grandmothers be role models for us? They look at us with bewilderment. Lena's mother can't comprehend her choice to leave her husband and have only one child. Alex's mother wrings her hands futilely and despairs at the pace of her daughter's life and the effects she believes it has on her grandchildren's well-being. One generation later, we have Allison's feminist mother, who cannot begin to understand her daughter's choice to get married instead of having a career.

This is a troublesome predicament that we have gotten ourselves into because it is difficult, if not impossible, for women to have a healthy female identity without some connection to a positive source of female role modeling. As a result, many women reach adulthood poorly equipped to deal with the challenges of relationships, personal achievement, mothering and self-esteem issues. We grope in the dark for adequate female mentoring and support that could show us how to be strong, passionate women in the world we live in now.

This lack of mentoring and role modeling can be addressed, however, through groups of women who come together with the intention of healing and empowering each other. We can provide support, information and mirroring to one another. In essence, we become a minicommunity in which a full circle of women of all ages pools their resources to mentor one another, fill in the gaps of missing culture and delve deeply into the well of the feminine soul.

☀Fierce Beauty Tip

What did you learn about being a woman when you were growing up? In your Fierce Beauty journal make a list of all your beliefs about being a woman, both positive and negative. Who or what were the sources of your information? Identify the most reliable source of positive input.

Initiation into the Feminine Soul

There are many styles and variations of female initiation practices around the world, particularly in nontechnologically oriented tribal cultures. Traditionally, initiation ceremonies would involve a series of highly ritualized activities designed to separate a young woman from her child self and to help her make the transition to her woman self. She would be taken from her family, and with other young women, have to meet certain challenges and perform ritual tasks. She would receive instruction from her elders about not only the practical affairs of daily life, but also her role in tending the spiritual life of her community. The person who emerged from the initiation rite was reborn again, not as a child to her mother, but as a woman to her people.

A woman who undergoes such a process knows herself and knows her relationship to the world around her. She knows that she is essential to her community, inextricably woven into its fabric. She also finds her own relationship to the spiritual world. From the perspective of indigenous cultures, those of us who grow up in technological societies without being held by the container of strong ceremonial practice, are only half-formed child adults. The Mescalero Apaches believe that their puberty rites are crucial, not only for the young woman, but for the health of the tribe. In her strength lies the strength of the people.

We had the opportunity in our group to create ourselves anew. We could use the focused container of the group to provide a unique, contemporary and relevant initiatory experience that, step by step, could take the unformed, unrooted child parts of us and grow them into womanhood. As in all initiations, that would require stepping away from our familiar world, being stripped of our old sense of self, meeting difficult challenges at times and, finally, accepting the responsibility to give the gifts of our fierce femininity back to the community.

"How can a group like this be a replacement for a traditional form of initiation?" asked Sylvia.

"The form is, of course, very different," I responded, "but there are basic elements of initiation that our group can provide. An initiation ceremony is a sacred event, with certain rules and protocols that build the ritual container. In a similar way, we can think of our group as being a special or sacred space. We can create that safe space with ground rules, like confidentiality, for example. Nothing said in the group leaves the group. That's essential for us to build trust.

"Often when a young girl is initiated," I went on, "she leaves her family and lives separately with other initiates for a while. During that time, the older women will teach her about being a woman. When we come here, we are separating from the rest of our lives. In this time and space, we are in a kind of free zone, where we can let go of our daily concerns for a bit and express ourselves in ways that we might not ordinarily feel comfortable doing."

"We're lucky," Sophie declared. "In our group, we have three generations of women. We learn from each other's experience."

"It's a great opportunity," I agreed. "Each generation has its own set of obstacles and blessings. I'm especially glad we have Elinor here to be our elder."

"Oh, I like this," she responded, with a chuckle. "So I can tell everyone what to do and they'll actually listen?"

"Well, don't get too carried away," Lena said playfully. "We'll just have to see about this."

"We have a lot of gifts to share," I continued. "We can fill in some of the holes of qualities that may be missing in our everyday lives. Sometimes, one of us may need some nurturing and compassion. Other times, we might need some fierce but loving confrontation."

"I'd like to think of us as a learning community," suggested Sophie, "aspiring to expand our horizons. I'd like to go past what I know about myself and become something more. I suspect that all of you could help me do this." She looked thoughtfully at the rest of us.

"It sounds like initiations are essentially birthing processes," Elinor said. "I used to work in obstetrics when I was a nurse. There was nothing more precious than helping those babies arrive. In a similar way, I think we can be midwives, welcoming and receiving each other into the world."

✳Fierce Beauty Tip

Organize a ladies' salon. Pick a topic of conversation that is relevant to women's lives to be the focus of your event. Invite all the women you know, serve tea and cookies and enjoy a lively exchange of information and experience.

Fierce Beauty Rules!

I could see that the fire was growing low in the stove. The cookie plate had long since been relieved of its contents. The room had settled into a thoughtful but comfortable quietness. Outside in the distance, I could hear dogs barking and an occasional coyote heralding the moon.

"I think we need a name," said Sylvia, "something that describes who we are."

"Yeah, what shall we call us?" asked Allison, sleepily. She had curled up like a cat on a pillow on the floor near Elinor's feet.

"I once heard a woman at a conference mention in passing the idea of fierce beauty," I shared. "I don't know what she meant by it, but it touched my imagination. I like the idea of feeling both beautiful and fierce at the same time. Usually we're either one or the other—passive decorative women prissing and preening in an endless obsession with our looks, or non-beautiful, nonsensual, unfeminine women who are tough and capable. I'd like to be feminine and strong. I want to love my womanhood in all its parts, and I know I have a long way to go to do that. But let's pick a name that affirms the best of who we are."

"I like it," said Lena. "I like the idea of being fierce. It reminds me of being wild and in nature, like being a wild animal that fiercely protects her babies, or her home. There's something elemental about it."

"I feel a long ways from being a fierce beauty, in any sense of the word, but I like the idea of it," agreed Jenny.

"Well, that could be a goal for our group—for each one of us to feel like fierce beauties as we go through our lives," suggested Alex.

"Can an old woman like me be a fierce beauty?" teased Elinor.

"Absolutely," said Sophie emphatically. "We're taking back the word and giving it new life and new meaning. I don't think fierce beauty is bound by age or the physical body. You are one of the loveliest 'old ladies' I've ever seen."

"Well, how about the Fierce Beauty Club?" I proposed.

"I like it. It's a little mysterious. People will wonder what it means, but it's kind of evocative," Lena mused.

And so the journey began. We were already discovering that, through witnessing each other's pain and joy, and telling the truth of our experience, something very special was happening. We were no longer the enemy. Competition and distrust were melting away and being replaced with acceptance and encouragement. We were creating a safe container in which the broken parts of us could begin to heal, the withered parts begin to thrive again and the flowers that had been dormant for so long begin to bloom.

· · ·

STEP 1: Create regular, ongoing connections with your women friends.

CHAPTER 2

Stepping into Our Feminine Power

Our deepest fear is not that we are inadequate,
our deepest fear is that we are powerful beyond
measure.
                                    —Nelson Mandela

IT WAS POURING outside, as the Fierce Beauties arrived one by one, shaking themselves off like wet dogs as they came in the door. Sophie looked nervously at her ceiling saying, "I hope the roofing patch that Michael and I put on last weekend holds." She passed around hot steaming cups of tea, which were vigorously welcomed by the sodden crew.

We were just getting started when Jenny burst in, slamming the door shut behind her against the wind-driven rain. Her eyes were red and swollen and she was in an obvious state of distress. Tears ran down her face, blotched with eye makeup. Wet strands of hair were clinging limply to her cheeks. "I just found out that Sam's having an affair with one of his co-workers. I found a letter that she wrote to him in his pants' pocket," she wailed. "I can't believe it. I gave everything to him," she cried. "I fixed his dinner every night. I listened endlessly while he whined about his problems. I went to the gym three times a week to try and stay in shape. I tried my very best to be a good mother and a good wife." Her voice rose as she began to sob. "I did exactly what everyone expected of me and this is what happens!"

Jenny's already fragile self-esteem was crashing down in shards all around her. As she continued to weep, several women gathered round her, softly murmuring words of comfort. Lena took her hand and led her over to the couch. She sat down, pulled Jenny close and just holding her, rocked slowly back and forth. The room was silent except for the sounds of the rain drumming on the roof and Jenny's keening.

As Jenny's sobbing gradually stopped, we began to talk about our relationships. Provoked by Jenny's pain, the conversation turned toward our individual and collective wounds from men. A river of grief opened up in the group, like the rain rushing rapidly downhill. The hurt and anger of most women is never far from the surface. It takes little impetus for us to find ourselves returning repeatedly to our unhealed wounds.

It is a rare woman today who cannot recite a number of commonly held beliefs about the unfair predicaments of women in our culture and around the world. We know the statistics about sexual assault, domestic violence, and educational and pay inequities for women. Most of us have felt tyrannized by our insane beauty standards. And many women have, at some point, felt betrayed, exploited, abused or, at the very least, unloved or disrespected by men in their lives.

Sophie looked increasingly uncomfortable as we went on recounting our negative experiences with men. As Lena was going on loudly about the "jerk" that was her last date, Sophie objected. "Wait a minute," she exclaimed. "I know this is a horrible thing for Jenny, but I don't feel right about what we're doing. I've spent years feeling like a victim and blaming other people for my problems. First my parents, then my boyfriends, and then finally all men. Haven't we done this long enough? I came to this group for something different."

"I agree," Elinor answered. "This feels like same old, same old. I know it's important to 'feel our pain,' but I'd like to learn how to change some of these problems for the better. Most of the women I know have been stuck in their hurt and their anger for years and complaining to each other hasn't really helped all that much. Can't we move on from here?"

Turning the Tide on Victim Psychology

Most women have learned a great deal in the past decades about our victimization, the lack of opportunities available, what we don't have and what we *aren't* supposed to be any more. In many ways, women's identity has become defined more by the shape of our wounds than by the presence of our gifts. I've witnessed sisterhood evoked more often through the awareness of common pain than through celebrations of the power, presence and beauty of womanhood. Psychologist Rollo May suggests that, "There is one way of confronting one's powerlessness—by making it a seeming virtue." In her book, *Fire with Fire*, Naomi Wolf writes that "victim feminism is when a woman seeks power through an identity of powerlessness."

The polarized psychology of victimhood idealizes women as the occupants of our culture's moral high ground and assumes that men are morally inferior. We've developed a social equation in which men are seen as having the power and are guilty of its misuse; women are imagined as powerless and innocent of all wrongdoing. All bad things that happen in our world are the purview of men and masculinity. All good things are part of women and femininity.

"But Liz," argued Sylvia, "women have been the ones who were cast as the bad guys for a long time. The Bible blames Eve for getting us kicked out of the Garden of Eden. Plato didn't even think women had souls! Don't you think turnabout is fair play? I think it's about time we were on top for a while.

"I'm discriminated against all the time at work. Most men don't take me seriously because I'm a woman. I've had times where they ignored my ideas and then when some guy came up with the same plan, it's like they heard it for the first time. It infuriates me." She got up and started pacing agitatedly around the room.

"So we should stoop so low?" retorted Sophie, tossing more wood onto the fire. "When do we show some leadership and take the whole mess to a new level?"

I responded, saying, "I know a lot of women feel the way you do, Sylvia. What I believe, though, is that while our pain and our anger about our wounds are an important place to visit, they are not a very good place to live in.

"I think this myth of female powerlessness is very destructive to women's healing," I continued. "It robs us of knowing ourselves as powerful, potent creators of own destinies. It's a bottomless chasm out of which women's true power and sense of worth just seep away. Victimhood creates the illusion that we have no responsibility or even capacity to change, because the problem lies outside of us. This way of thinking is clearly divisive to our relationships with men, but it harms us more."

"What kind of message are we teaching our daughters?" asked Elinor. "That they have no power? That they're victims of some huge, nebulous conspiracy of men? How can they find their way through that maze?"

"I don't understand what you're all talking about," Jenny said vehemently, "The truth is, I *feel* totally powerless right now. I don't have a lot of money. I'm not important. I don't have any influence in the world; I certainly don't have any influence over my husband. He did this to *me*, I am the victim here," she argued.

"Sam did something lousy and hurtful," I responded. "But you have the power over your own response. Nobody—not Sam, your kids or anybody else, can take away your sense of worth and power. Your power comes from you, and only you can give it away or lose it."

Sylvia continued pacing around, obviously upset with the way the conversation was headed. "Isn't this what they call 'blaming the victim'?" she said to me, her face flushed with anger. "What did Jenny have to do with this? Sam broke her heart. He acted like a pig! She didn't do anything wrong."

"It's not about someone being wrong or right," I answered slowly, trying to find the right words. "If Jenny's well-being is all in the hands of Sam, then she has no power. If he's good to her, then she's happy. If he's bad to her, she's miserable. But if she's in charge of her own experience, then she knows that *she* can make it better or worse. It means that Jenny can choose to not reject herself, even if Sam has rejected her.

"You have no control over Sam, you can't fix him," I offered, turning to look directly at Jenny. "You do have control over yourself. You can fix you."

"It's true I've been childish in certain ways," she reflected. "I've been trying to please Sam, like a little kid trying to make daddy happy. All my attention has been on what he wants and needs. It would probably be good for me to start focusing on myself for awhile."

☀Fierce Beauty Tip

In what part of your life do you give your power away? Who are you waiting for to change so that your life can improve? Make a list of the things that you can do to enhance the quality of your existence. Start with small, but significant actions.

Revealing the Hidden Power of Women

One of the reasons that women often think or feel that they are not powerful is the ways in which we define power. Many of us see power as gaining dominance over others—the ability to control resources and people. Power is also associated with physical strength, having a large public presence, influence or a great deal of money. And, in fact, many women still do not have as much access to these types of power as men. But this definition of power overlooks the various kinds of power that we do have.

This issue came to my attention a number of years ago when I was co-teaching gender communications seminars around the country with my husband, Aaron. The participants frequently scrutinized us heavily for any possible signs of inequity in our relationship. Periodically, some woman would come up to us afterward and mention that she had actually timed the intervals that we each talked and noticed that Aaron had talked longer than I had. We both dreaded these confrontations, which implied that Aaron was oppressing me and that I was being oppressed. We would both feel demeaned and insulted.

To preemptively avoid such incidents we began carefully timing all of our lectures. I felt constant pressure to talk as much as Aaron when we were in public. It then occurred to me that I was attempting to eliminate any gender difference between us in order to appear to be more "equal." A friend helpfully pointed out to me that she thought I held space in a very different way than Aaron did when we taught together. There were fewer words spoken in that space, but an equal amount of presence. She observed that I had a spiritual and compassionate presence that strongly affected the atmosphere and the positive outcome of our trainings. I realized that when I talked less, I was able to pay closer attention to the dynamics of the group. I could access my intuition more readily about what was needed for the group. After we tried this new approach, participants commented that they enjoyed our complementary teaching styles.

Now I encourage women and men who participate in our workshops to consider the lens through which we view power. Could it be that women's power is sometimes less external than men's? Less visible and definable in terms of actions or products? In *Women's Worth*, Marianne Williamson writes,

"Today, the reason we haven't found our grail, the key to who we are as women, is because we look for it in worlds of false power, the very worlds that took it away from us in the beginning."

Many women are deeply influenced by models of male empowerment. One of the primary models for women claiming power in the world is what Jungians would call the "animus driven" woman. Inner masculinity, however, has the potential to infect women's psyches with the same dysfunctional behaviors and attitudes associated with a male sex role model that is, in many ways, toxic to men. Aspiring to a male model of power can also breed resentment in women—we can never be as good as men at being men. Consequently, when we play their game by their rules, we do so with a handicap. Trying to use masculinity as the cure for feminine wounds is like trying to get rid of a headache by listening to loud music. It rarely succeeds.

In *The Princessa: Machiavelli for Women*, Harriet Rubin suggests that, "For a woman to triumph, she cannot play by the rules of the game. They are not her rules, designed to enhance her strengths. She has to change the game." One way that we change the game is through taking ownership of our authentic female authority through stepping outside the known world of power and recreating it according to our own feminine strategic sensibilities.

Just as there are public and private expressions of creativity, there are also public and private expressions of power. Traditionally, women, for the most part, tended to wield power privately and from behind the scenes. Anthropologist Helen Fisher discovered that even in matrilineal cultures, where descent is traced through the mother and women hold the bulk of property and wealth (approximately 15 percent of all human societies), women do not hold public positions of leadership. In most hunter-gatherer societies throughout time, women have enjoyed substantial power, but rarely displayed this power publicly. Women's power is like gravity; you can't see it, but it holds the world together.

In our culture we know this phenomena as the "woman behind the throne." The vast majority of men in visible positions of power, from CEOs to senators, are married. Single men rarely achieve this level of success. The wives of married men are cocreators in the achievement of their family's economic and political power. They can enable their partners to soar. Women are kingmakers. Now, however, we want to be recognized as queens in our own right, sharing the throne in full partnership.

Fierce Beauty Tip

Is there a way in which you may be powerful that you are unaware of? Starting with the words, "I feel powerful when . . ." write down a list of the ways you express your power in your daily life.

Emotional Power

The issue of male and female power often comes up in our gender communication workshops, where we provide an opportunity for women and men to give each other information about one another's behavior. One day a man stood up, after listening to the women speak at length about their shared sense of powerlessness, and declared that, in his experience, he thought women were extremely powerful. When the other men were polled on this point, they agreed wholeheartedly that they perceived the women in their lives as being very powerful. In fact, the majority claimed that the most powerful person who personally influenced their lives was a woman. The women were very surprised to hear this feedback from men. "Why then is there such a discrepancy in our perceptions?" one of the women asked.

Men experience women as being "emotionally" powerful. To them, we are tidal waves of emotionality, hurricanes of mood. From the time they are small boys, mostly they are at the mercy of their mothers, who seem very large to them. But as men become adults, often not much changes. Although their bodies are bigger, they still, at times, feel at the mercy of the enormous power of women's emotionality and can be easily flooded and overwhelmed by women's feelings.

One reason for this difference lies in the socialization of boys and girls. When boys grow up they are taught to numb out their feelings, to "take it like a man, and don't cry, be a big boy." This systematic desensitization, which is part of training men to adopt a role in which they are willing to face danger, often has the end result of creating adult men who have suppressed their emotions for years. Girls, on the other hand, are generally encouraged to be in touch with their feelings and to readily express them. As a result, most women reach adulthood with much stronger emotional "muscles" than men. Nature endowed men with larger physical muscle mass, but compensated women with stronger emotional mass.

I've noticed in my relationship with Aaron that when I move through my lunar cycle, he is deeply affected by my changes in mood. As I become premenstrual and the tidal waters of my unconscious flood, he in turn sometimes becomes flooded as well. No matter how well I attempt to contain my moods, he is affected. This phenomenon may be one of the reasons that women in many different cultures around the world intentionally withdrew from communal activities during menses. The emotional pull in a woman's psyche is exceptionally strong during this period, and has profound effects on the people around her.

We swim in the turbulent sea of our emotions all the time. But what is normal and commonplace to many women is often not to men, many of whom find our tears terrifying and our rage intimidating. Much of men's efforts to control women or separate from them may stem more from their inability to defend themselves adequately from our emotional power than from a patriarchal conspiracy. But, just as it's essential for men to learn to manage their anger, it is important for women to become aware of the emotional power that we wield and to learn how to manage it with integrity.

Fierce Beauty Tip

Explore the effects of your emotional power on the people closest to you. Notice the ways in which the intensity of your emotion, be it joy, grief or anger, affects the moods of others. If you are in an intimate relationship with a man, ask him to tell you when and how he experiences your emotional power.

Relationship Power

"Women more often see power as a network of vital human connection," writes Helen Fisher in *The First Sex*. Fisher regards the power of women to create relationships, which are the building blocks of community, as a profoundly important force in the world. Our passions for relating to others, as well as our skills in negotiating and sustaining relationships are a needed ingredient for humanizing our business and political institutions. The movements in business toward "lateral" rather than hierarchical organization, and an emphasis on mutually cooperative teamwork, are indications of a growing trend to incorporate women's relationship power into the marketplace.

Women's ability to create and sustain human connection is essential to keeping families and communities together. It provides a source of strength and support that is as necessary to humans as food and water. The fact that women have access to this web of nurturing relationship gives them a form of power and strength that often eludes men. Men may be making more money, but are, in fact, usually far more isolated.

We can see this graphically illustrated with divorce. After divorce, women's economic well-being takes a downward turn, but men's emotional health crashes. Their suicide rate doubles. They frequently lose access to the web of human connection and support provided by their wife. Children and social networks usually exit with the wife. Most men have few relationship resources of their own, often depending solely on their wife or girlfriend to meet their needs for intimacy. This may be one of the reasons that married men live longer and have overall better physical and mental health than single men.

Just as there are many kinds of wealth, there are many forms of power. Relationships are women's gold. They are the food we nurture ourselves and others with in order to sustain life. Successful relationships, whether with children, lovers, friends or family, require the use of many skills. Women with relationship power both know the essential value of their relationships and have the willingness to tend them like gardens that will someday bear fruit. This tending requires ongoing focus and infinite patience—skills practiced by women during child rearing since the beginning of time.

Fierce Beauty Tip

Make a list of your relationship assets both at work and in your personal life. How much "relationship gold" have you acquired, and how do these assets enhance the quality of your life?

Nurturing Power

I recently gave a presentation at a national women's conference on this topic of women's power. During the workshop I asked women to stand up and share with the audience their personal experiences of being powerful. A number of the participants told us about situations in which they felt they had the power to transform other people with love. This potent force, which has profound effects on individuals and society at large, could be called "nurturing" power. Marianne Williamson declares that, "We don't have to give birth to children to know that we are the mothers of the world."

Women nurture. It doesn't matter whether we are tending children, men, community and church groups, boardrooms, international affairs, students, clients or customers or each other. The dictionary defines nurture as "the act or process of promoting growth." It derives from the same root word as nurse and nourish, which also relate to the sustaining of life. We do ourselves a great disservice when we ignore or demean the potency of this kind of power. Our capacity to make human systems whole, maintain families and serve communities creates enduring cohesion and ensures the psychological survival of our species.

Nurturing power is difficult to measure, but we know well the effects of its absence. As women choose to nurture less and place their energies elsewhere, children and families often suffer consequences to their well-being. As a society, we clearly need to continue to support women's desire to pursue avenues of expression outside nurturing roles. It is not the all of who we are. But we have yet to reconstruct our social fabric in a way that adequately replaces women's nurturing power when it is absent.

Fierce Beauty Tip

Think about who or what you nurture with the empowering love of your heart. How do you see these people and projects flowering in response to this gift? Give yourself praise for your valuable contribution.

Verbal Power

Women also are endowed with strong verbal power, which can be seen as a gift, particularly in an information age that places a high premium on the ability to communicate. Women are actually physiologically structured to have a verbal advantage over men. The left cortex of the brain, which contains the verbal centers, develops later in males, and the *corpus callosum* that links the brain's two hemispheres is thicker in women. Much has been written about the significance of the difference in size and thickness of the *corpus callosum* in men and women. Most important, the larger *corpus callosum* in women appears to facilitate more connection between different areas of the brain, what Fisher calls "web thinking" or a multimodal processing of image and language.

Girls talk earlier than boys. As they learn to form language, they make longer word chains and sentences. They have better vocabulary skills and a dramatically lower incidence of verbal difficulties, such as stuttering and dyslexia. Boys have three times the level of reading difficulties of girls. Girls test higher in verbal skills throughout school, performing better than boys in language and writing classes by far.

By the time we become adults, women talk, on average, twice as many words a day as men. The one exception to this is that women talk less in public than men. Linguist Deborah Tannen has done extensive research into gender differences in communication. She concludes that women engage in "rapport talk" designed to enhance their connections with others, whereas men are more likely to use "report talk" to communicate information. Women's verbal power is also somewhat linked with the rise and fall of estrogen during menstrual cycles. When estrogen levels rise, women become more articulate due to an increase in the amount of dendritic connections on the neurons in our brains.

Men report that they often feel verbally outgunned by

women during relationship confrontations. Many women have quicker access to feelings and better ability to articulate those feelings. We also have a greater tolerance for sustaining engagement around relationship issues than men. We are willing to hang in there way beyond the point that men have exhausted their reserves of emotional and verbal power. Women can abuse their linguistic power by becoming verbally abusive and shaming to others. Language is a sword we know how to use well. We can tear another person to shreds with the power of our words, or we can use this power to create connections and build bridges.

☀ Fierce Beauty Tip

Where in your life do you use your powerful word sword? Notice if you are building up or tearing down the people around you with this potent tool.

Influence Power

Another form of power that women have wielded throughout time is influence power. On a grand scale this is the power to change the course of evolution. Females of many species affect the course of evolution through their reproductive choices. Science writer and researcher Mary Batten in her book, *Sexual Strategies: How Females Choose Their Mates*, suggests that, "female choice, whether individual or familial, played a major role, not only in determining how males look and act, but also in influencing cultural value systems, social structures, and the laws and customs for governing and maintaining those structures."

This perspective on the evolution of human behavior, shared by many biologists, anthropologists and evolutionary psychologists, flies in the face of the proponents of victim feminism.

Scientific inquiry has shown that the females of most species select the more dominant, aggressive males, who have proven their protective viability through various competitive strategies. They do not choose males who are tender, sensitive or compassionate. It appears that much of the behavior that we criticize in men is, in fact, behavior that females have desired and rewarded for hundreds of thousands of years.

In a more immediate sphere of influence, women, as the primary socializers of children, are the ones who hold much of the power to shape the actions of generations to come. Of course, women alone do not entirely control the behaviors of their children. There are also fathers, educators, peers and others. Nonetheless, women remain the main caretakers of children as well as the vast majority of primary and secondary school teachers. We have an instrumental role in socialization and have exerted this power since our ancestors sat around fires clothed in skins. We exercise this power not only with children, but also with the men in our lives. We affect change by the choices we make and the kinds of behaviors we encourage.

☀ Fierce Beauty Tip

Make a list of the people you influence and the ways you affect their behaviors and attitudes. Are you pleased with the legacy of your influence power? If so, give yourself the recognition and appreciation you deserve.

Sexual Power

Not all women have access to beauty and sexual power, but for those who do, it is a potent force. The existence of women's sexual power is evidenced by historical and contemporary attempts worldwide to contain and control women's sexuality. Chastity belts, clitoridectomies, the use of veiling in Muslim cultures, as well as extensive societal taboos and rules, regulate women's sexual behavior. According to Geraldine Brooks in *Nine Parts of Desire*, the impulse to heavily restrict Muslim women's behavior stems from a deep-seated fear in men of their sexual power. Islamic teaching says "Almighty God created sexual desire in ten parts; then he gave nine parts to women and one to men."

Historically, men in many different parts of the world have regarded women's sexuality as a dangerous force that needed to be controlled. In fact, men *are* extraordinarily vulnerable to our sexual power. When under its influence, they can lose all ability to think clearly, make rational choices and be responsible to the people they love. Sometimes seemingly otherwise sensible men destroy their lives over a woman's sexual allure.

A common theme in movies and television is that of the *femme fatale*, a beautiful woman who uses her sexuality to seduce, control or destroy some man. Her sexual power is a tool, not unlike a weapon, that can be used to manipulate men and achieve her desired end. Her goal may be money, political influence, economic power or the destruction of a government. History is rich with stories of powerful women who changed the course of events with their sexual power. Cleopatra used her sexuality to enchant and seduce Julius Caesar and Marc Antony, thereby challenging the entire Roman Empire. Delilah, whose name translates to "She Who Makes Weak," destroyed Samson. President Bill Clinton's administration was nearly toppled by a sensual young woman in thong underwear.

Sexual power, however, is a mixed bag for a variety of reasons. Many women feel they have limited access to it, because they lack the requisite type of physical beauty in vogue today. This kind of beauty is also limited and transitory by nature. It exists, however, as a sort of default program for women. When in doubt, manipulate with your sexuality. Women are often taught by their mothers to use their beauty power to catch a man who will take care of them.

Regardless of the shadow of this form of feminine power, it

cannot be overlooked in an exploration of women's power. It's useful for us to examine and understand its baggage and the way it's been misused against both men and women. But we've got it, girlfriends, and we use it whenever we can. Sexual power can be as destructive as military power, but it is also a force of nature that ensures the survival of the human species.

☀️Fierce Beauty Tip

Are there people in your personal or professional life that you have influenced with your sexual power in order to achieve your desires? Make a list of the specific behaviors that you used to accomplish this, including the way you dress and move your body.

Intuitive Power

When I was traveling in Greece a few years ago, I had the privilege of visiting Delphi, one of the spiritual centers of the ancient world. Pilgrims from many places traveled to Delphi to consult the Delphic oracle, the Pythoness, who lived in a cave and was believed to be a conduit for the wisdom of Apollo, the sun god. Before becoming the domain of this powerful deity, however, Delphi was home to an ancient earth oracle, Delphyne, the Womb of Creation. The shrine, sacred to the earth mother, was tended by elderly women priestesses whose oracular wisdom guided the community in its daily affairs. The prophecies and visions of this ancient feminine oracle played a significant role in the religious, economic and political affairs of that part of the world well into the fourth century, when the oracle stopped speaking forever saying:

"Tell the King, the fairwrought hall has fallen to the ground, no longer has Phoebus a hut or a prophetic laurel, nor a spring that speaks. The water of speech even is quenched."

As with women's verbal skills, there are also biological structures in our brains that contribute to the phenomena known as women's intuition. Our well-developed corpus callosum with its myriad connections among different areas of the brain makes it possible for women to access complex kinds of information. This "bilateralized" functioning gives us the neural pathways that make possible the insight that we think of as "women's intuition." Various studies demonstrate that women can better recognize subtle nuances of expression on people's faces and identify the accompanying emotions than men. Women are also able to hear better than men, and recognize complex audio cues that provide information about a person's emotional state.

Undoubtedly, we developed these abilities in order to effectively respond to the needs of children and families. We've learned to fine-tune our perceptions to be able to know what the people around us need. This intuitive skill is a power that women have that increases with age. The old wise woman who uses her female intuition and wisdom to enrich her people is a universal archetype.

Fierce Beauty Tip

Access your inner "wise woman" to expand your intuitive power. First, identify a question that you have. Then, sitting in a quiet place, allow your mind to drift gently and softly. No effort is required. Just be receptive to the deep voices within you and notice what spontaneously comes.

Self-Actualizing Power

Perhaps the most important form of power available to all women is self-actualizing power. The word "power" comes from the Latin word, *posse*, which means, "to be able." Power, from this perspective, is about capacity and ability. Nietzsche's famous line, "Wherever I found the living, I found the will to power," refers to the basic human drive to survive, persevere and make a place for themselves in the world. To have power is to succeed in being able to live well—to thrive.

Author Warren Farrell, in *Why Men Are the Way They Are*, writes that, "When we say that 'men have all the power,' we reinforce the assumption that income, status and control over others are more important than assessing our values internally . . . that external reward is all there is to power." He lists a variety of different kinds of power that have to do with the ability to create a fulfilling life on one's own terms that include: access to external rewards and resources, access to internal rewards and resources, access to interpersonal contact, access to physical health, attractiveness, and intelligence equivalent to one's expectation or desire, and access to sexual fulfillment.

Self-actualizing power, for both sexes, means breaking out of limiting social and familial programs that dictate the scope of what we will allow ourselves to dream about and create. Both men and women are trained to uphold certain roles that may enhance the collective, but not necessarily the individual's soul. Self-actualizing power gives us the capacity to change our lives to accurately reflect the truth of who we are. It is the capacity to pursue health at all levels and to have goals that we follow through on.

☀ Fierce Beauty Tip

With the help of a close woman friend, choose a goal that you would like to achieve. Make a pact to help each other reach your goals through making commitments to one another to follow through on your action strategies. Check on each other's progress at regular intervals.

We Are Powerful and Feminine at the Same Time

After a lively discussion on the many different kinds of power, the group fell silent, contemplating what we'd been talking about. The rain had stopped its incessant drumming on the roof, and a chorus of frogs began righteously exercising their freedom of speech.

"Wow," exclaimed Alex, finally breaking the spell, "I never really considered power in that way. I guess I've always imagined power as being masculine, and if I want to be powerful, I need to do like what men do. But this opens up whole other realms of possibility."

"Yeah," agreed Sylvia. "You know, my father was a powerful man. He commanded a lot of authority. I always worshipped him. My mother seemed so weak and pitiful in comparison that I've tried to imitate him my whole life. The world of engineering is very male, and I've tried to fit myself into their idea of capability. It never occurred to me before that my definition of power was so influenced by male culture."

There is no limitation to the many kinds of power available to women. We can be anything we choose to be. The world is slowly opening up doors and arenas that were previously closed. But women can create dominion in uniquely feminine ways, moving into male domains without losing their connection with their essential female being. Fierce femininity is a quality embodied by women who have developed their strength and presence. Fierce Beauties actualize their dreams and take control of their lives while staying connected with their feminine souls. Our work is to fill ourselves up with ourselves and let loose upon the world the undeniable truth of who we are. Therein lies our power.

As we continued talking that night, the Fierce Beauties decided to rethink our old concepts about power and start imagining ourselves as being powerful. We started looking around our lives for women who we felt embodied this ideal that could inspire us. I suggested to the group that in the weeks ahead,we also look closely at our own behaviors to become aware of our victim patterns, as well as the ways that we wielded power in our lives.

☀ Fierce Beauty Tip

Imagine that your female body is a container or vessel. Fill this vessel with the essence of your fierce beauty. From your toes to your fingertips to the top of your head, occupy each cell and nerve ending. Then imagine your essence moving beyond your body and becoming an expanding luminous glow.

Old Habits and False Power

A couple weeks later we met again on a Sunday afternoon. The winter rains were finally letting up and spring was in the air. The sun sparkled, wildflowers bloomed and life seemed full of rampant possibility. We chatted awhile informally, making connections and checking in with each other about the state of our lives. Sylvia and Allison were both involved in a long-distance walk for women to raise money to fight breast cancer. They were passing out brochures and looking for sponsors. Sophie showed me her latest piece. She was working on a series of paintings of her grandmother.

We settled down after a bit. We were all anxious to hear from Jenny about how things were going with her and Sam.

"Things are very tense at home, as you can imagine," she explained. "We're sleeping in different rooms and I'm so angry at him that I can hardly bear to see him. The children are upset. But at least he's willing to try and work on our relationship. He feels pretty horrible about what happened and has agreed to stop seeing this woman, at least while we sort out our situation. We've started going to a counselor through our church.

She's having us take a look at what we each contributed to things getting so bad between us—what she calls 'our 50 percent.' It goes right along with what we've been talking about in the group.

"I've been looking at the ways that I misuse my power. At first I thought I didn't have any. But after our last discussion I realized that I do use power to get the people around me to do what I want. But the way I do it is very convoluted. When I don't get what I want I withdraw into sort of a resentful silence. I just put out bad vibes, kind of like a black cloud that hangs around like a smelly fart. Or I snipe at Sam from the sidelines, making little nasty jibes and sarcastic comments.

"I have these oblique ways of communicating to him that I'm unhappy. But I've never, until the counseling sessions, said clearly and directly to him what I wanted and needed."

Because women are so strongly encouraged to serve other people, we often tend to submerge our needs. But submerged needs become subversive. Our will to power moves into life in any way that it can. We have traditionally influenced and controlled the people and environments around us indirectly through the use of various forms of manipulation power.

THE SULKER

One form of manipulation power is the power of silence. We've probably all had the experience of being at the mercy of a person who refused to communicate verbally and just projected a loaded and hostile silence—"the sulker." The sulker's power is based on nonverbal techniques of communication that include facial scowls, grimaces, tightened lips, and heavy sighs. The sulker withdraws verbally, but not energetically.

THE MARTYR

Another form of manipulation power many women use is our old friend, "the martyr." The martyr wields power through guilt. She lets the people around her know in subtle ways that they are falling short of her expectations. The martyr has effaced her own needs for the sake of others. She is a codependent victim who wears a mask of willing service to others, but, in fact, is deeply angered at her own neglect. She is caught in blaming others, sticking them with the responsibility to magically interpret the hidden code of her language of guilt.

THE CASTIGATOR

Another form of negative power familiar to many of us is "the castigator." The castigator has well-developed verbal skills and uses her tongue like a sword. Feeling insufficient herself, she projects that insufficiency onto others through making them feel small and inadequate. This can happen through a torrent of tongue-lashing or small jabs of spite. Either way, the castigator uses shame as her weapon, reducing the self-worth of the people around her.

Embracing fierce femininity entails a rigorous examination of the ways that we have unconsciously manipulated others instead of cleanly and clearly asking for what we wanted. It also requires that we find ways to extricate ourselves from old patterns of domination and submission. Becoming fierce beauties means that we are stepping out of these dysfunctional patterns into more equitable and meaningful partnerships with the significant people in our lives.

☀ Fierce Beauty Tip

What is your unique style of negative power? Pay attention to the indirect methods you use to get what you want. Start tracking your habitual patterns of reacting to frustrating situations. Make a list with two columns: the first column is a list of your wants and needs. The second column is a list of clear, direct actions that you can take to achieve your desires.

Strategies for Power

"I hardly ever feel powerful," Allison admitted. "Mostly, I wish that Billy would pay more attention to me. I start thinking about it as soon as I get up in the morning. I wonder if he really loves me and what I could do to get him to spend more time with me."

"Have you actually outright asked him for what you wanted?" suggested Elinor.

"He should know, it's obvious isn't it?"

"Apparently not," Elinor answered. "I think a lot of men aren't as good as women at picking up subtle cues. My husband always reminded me that he couldn't read my mind. He told me if I wanted something from him that I had to hit him right between the eyes with it."

"Most of your focus seems to be on changing him so that he can make you feel more loved," Sophie observed. "What happens if you pay attention to how you make *yourself* feel special and wanted? Like with Jenny, you may not be able to change him, but you can change yourself."

Changing old habits of powerlessness is not an easy task. It takes commitment, discipline and regular support. The first challenge was to change our beliefs about power and our attachment to being victims. Then we explored the shadow of women's power. Now we could get down to the nitty-gritty of how we actually begin to live as powerful, fiercely feminine women.

Power begins with assuming control of our own lives. That means we get up every day, and instead of expecting things from other people, we expect them from ourselves. We become the ones in charge of our joy, our play, our relaxation, our freedom and our autonomy of expression. One of the ways this is accomplished is through creating a plan for self-care. In this plan we develop strategies to maintain our physical, emotional and spiritual health. It requires understanding your organism well enough to anticipate and be responsive to its needs.

To stand in a place of power, you have to know what you want. Harriet Rubin proclaims, "Desire rules the world!" The passion of knowing what we truly desire fills us with energy, propelling us forward. Women often have trouble knowing what they want. We can easily tell you what the people around us want; we've paid close attention to them. But we can neglect listening to our own hearts, and then we get lost in other people's dreams.

We also, at times, find ourselves complaining repeatedly about our problems to other women. While it's important to have supportive friends who we can confide in, we lose our power when endless wailing, or "whanking," as my younger daughter calls it, consumes our energy. In stories of Pacific Northwest tribal life, they say that if a woman sits in a group of friends and repeats her story of woe more than three times, the women move away from her and form a new circle. They refuse to continue listening to a woman who takes no action to improve her lot. Claiming our fierce femininity means reorganizing ourselves toward strategic acts and away from habitual passive despair.

When there are conflicts with other people, we can explore our responsibility for cocreating the problem, as Jenny was doing with her marriage, because 50 percent of any situation is usually of our own making and within our power to change. If we pick an area of our life that causes us difficulty, we can make a list of the ways that we contribute to the problem.

☀ Fierce Beauty Tip

Create a self-care program. What do you need on a daily basis for your physical, emotional and spiritual health? Knowing how to adequately care for yourself is a source of great power. Share your program with other women friends and ask them for support.

As women we have only just begun our journey toward truly understanding the depth and the breadth of our power. We have lost and obscured many parts of ourselves. But we are peeking behind the curtain, and what we find there is exciting.

The Fierce Beauties made a pact to help each other stay focused on our own lives instead of constantly focusing on the shortcomings of others. In this way we began to nurture the spark of our will to power—our feminine fire. Becoming accountable to ourselves and to other women friends for taking responsibility for the quality of our daily lives is a great place to begin. It is very helpful to find ongoing support for changing lifelong habitual patterns rooted in negativity and disappointment. We can be reminders for one another of the goals we want to accomplish, the strategies we need to achieve these goals and the power we each possess to create fulfilling lives.

☀Fierce Beauty Tip

Engage in a private bragging session by doing the following writing exercise: Starting with the words, "I am . . . ," describe yourself in the biggest and wildest superlatives possible.

. . .

STEP 2: Assert your unique style of fierce feminine power.

CHAPTER 3

Communing with the Goddesses

The wanderings of the Goddess carried her far,
*   yet each spring*
She returned with her doves to Cyprus for
*   Her sacred bath at Paphos.*
                    —Charlene Spretnek

LENA ARRIVED at the group one evening after being gone for a couple of weeks. She had taken a trip to the Yucatan peninsula in Mexico with a girlfriend from work. Wearing a white cotton dress decorated with brightly colored embroidery patterns, she looked relaxed and refreshed.

"We had the most wonderful time," she reported, handing out small woven bracelets as souvenirs to the other women. "It's a very interesting area. Not only are there incredible white sand beaches and a turquoise-green ocean to swim in, there's also ancient Mayan ruins everywhere. My family originally migrated from the state of Quintana Roo many years ago, before I was born. I wanted to go back there to see where my roots were. I especially enjoyed being around so many women with the same body type as me. I felt totally at home. While I was there, I also read a lot about the Mayan Indian culture. They have a rich spiritual tradition which, nowadays, has partially blended with Catholicism."

Lena showed us some traditional Mayan incense that she had brought back, called copal. She lit a round disc of charcoal with a lighter and placed a small sticky piece of white resinous material on it. As it heated it up, it began to smoke, emitting a sweet, slightly tangy smell. "This reminds me of being in church," she said. "The priests would swing incense holders filled with frankincense, which is very similar to copal.

"We went to one archeological site that was sacred to the Mayan goddess, Ixchel. In fact, the guide told us that this site was the primary center in the whole Caribbean area for this particular deity. Archeologists found hundreds of female figurines there, representing Ixchel. They originated from a widespread area that ranged from Guatemala to Northern Mexico. Nowadays they worship her as the Virgin of Guadalupe. There's a large shrine for her at the entrance. Ixchel was a special patron of women, who made pilgrimages to her sacred shrine to pray for fertility.

"We got to sit on top of a pyramid in a spot that the guide told us was where the priests used to meditate and make prayers. I had the most extraordinary experience of touching this sweet energy. It was like being in the presence of the essence of love and safety and compassion. I've had glimpses of this before when I've prayed to the Virgin Mary, but not this strongly."

We started to talk about our different religious upbringings. Most of us felt a sense of loss that the spiritual traditions we were raised in, for the most part, imagined God and divinity as male. Because female religious images were scarce in our culture, many of us grew up feeling that our femininity was neither sacred nor imbued with the same social and spiritual power as masculinity. In fact, women were often regarded as unclean, even evil. This bias contributes to an impoverishment in the female psyche, adding to women's low self-esteem.

The mythology of a culture has a powerful effect on the psychology of its members. The icons of spiritual authority also influence the ideals most honored in daily life. A number of studies by anthropologists indicate that cultures whose myth-ologies include a strong feminine deity, who creates life either alone or in partnership with a male deity, tend toward a greater equality in gender roles between the sexes. Cultures with a pre-dominately male hierarchical spiritual order tend to duplicate that order in mundane worldly affairs. This is not to say that women who worship in the Judeo-Christian and Islamic tradi-tions cannot find deep fulfillment and meaning in those traditions. But the missing presence of a spiritual female image remains a barrier to a sense of belonging and fulfillment for many women.

Many women have a yearning to feel that a part of them is sacred, eternally divine and worthy of reverence intrinsically. We desire to find ourselves positively reflected in creation myths, religious teachings and the sacred writings of the cul-ture in which we live. In the Fierce Beauty Club, we decided that our next task was to go in search of other sources of mytho-logical and theological information about women.

Over the last few decades, there has been a surge of inter-est in research into female archetypes. One of the most exciting revelations for me was the extraordinarily wide range of femi-nine expression embodied in different goddess images. I discovered that the male emphasis in Judeo-Christian and Islamic culture is actually not the norm. From a larger histori-cal and anthropological perspective, our religious imagination has produced a vast repertoire of myths and images of aspects of womanhood. These female archetypes are potentially rich sources for women's healing and empowerment. When we explore feminine archetypes, we are learning about the collec-tive historical legacy of female culture—the oral and written tradition of the Motherline.

Some women tell me they feel reluctant to explore sacred images of the feminine for fear that they will engage in "goddess worship." Investigating the legacy of the sacred feminine, however, does not imply that we need to start a new religion or kneel at the feet of new deities, only that we open our hearts and minds to a larger, more inclusive picture of history and spirituality. A friend of mine, who is a pious Jew, recently told me that, through her mythological explorations, she had "discovered her inner goddess." This epiphany brought her a sense of joy and a greater capacity to celebrate her own feminine nature.

Stepping Beyond the Looking Glass

Archetypal energies are larger than life, unbounded by history, personal circumstances and even physical limitations. They exist as elemental streams of energy that animate the natural world that we are a part of. We could imagine that within the person that is you, there is an essential energy pattern imbuing you with a particular form and expression of life. In the East African Yoruba tradition, archetypes are called "orisas." Orisas are forces of nature, sources that exist not only in nature but in our own bodies as well. Each orisa, in this tradition, also has its own preferred colors, music, foods, dances, and environments.

When we reclaim the sacred feminine, we expand our imagination and begin to know ourselves in a different way than before. We can explore the elemental nature of our being. We are more than our bodies, more than a product of social upbringing and cultural mores. We are also color, sound, and movement. If you allow yourself the freedom to imagine that you can be anything or anywhere, who are you and where do you find yourself? What is your natural habitat or domain? What do you have dominion over? This information, once we decide to go hunting for it, often reveals itself through images in both waking and sleeping dreams.

Find a comfortable place where you allow your mind and body to relax. Take some deep breaths, allowing the cares of your everyday world to melt away as you exhale. Imagine going to a special place like a temple that has a sacred quality. You can create this holy dwelling any way you want. It is a unique expression of your magic and divinity, the home of the goddess within you. Notice what you see, feel and do in this place. It is your very own and you can return whenever you like.

Because so many goddesses are identified by their relationship to some aspect of the natural world, we can often experience the archetypal feminine most directly through being in nature. Recognizing our inextricable connection with nature helps women to find their value and their place in the larger schema of the natural universe. When we go out to the ocean or to a waterfall in the forest, for example, we can tune into the presence of the sacred feminine and allow it to penetrate and touch our soul. We can find the natural contexts that evoke an experience of ourselves as sacred and as a part of something divine.

Another technique for discovering more about the archetypal feminine that influences us is to collect physical symbols and images from our environment. This process is done most effectively through allowing our intuition to guide us. We want to "see" through the eyes of the archetypal feminine rather than through the conscious mind. This can yield new information about our deep essential nature. We are surrounded by images as we move through our daily lives. Notice what objects and images attract your attention. They have a story to tell. There are many ways to collect or work with symbolic images. We can build altars, make art projects of many kinds, do photography, write in journals, go to fabric stores and visit museums.

Dancing with the Nature Goddesses

Quite synchronistically, our next meeting fell on the night of the full moon. The sun set and shortly thereafter, the moon began to rise. It was uncharacteristically warm and clear for Santa Barbara in the early summer. "Let's go down to the beach," suggested Allison. "I know a great place that I used to go to with my friends. We can make a bonfire, there's plenty of driftwood laying around."

"That's a fantastic idea," agreed Sylvia. "Let's go howl at the moon." Everyone else was enthusiastic about the plan so off we went to the beach. We piled into two cars, carrying blankets, bonfire makings, some bottles of juice and some snacks.

The beach was serene, with only a slight soft wind blowing. The rising moon cast a silver path across the sea. The lazy surf rose and fell hypnotically. We spread out across the beach, gathering wood. Sophie began to build the fire, crumpling newspaper and placing twigs carefully in a teepee shape over the paper. After a few unsuccessful tries, she lit it. As it started to burn, she cupped her hands around the small flames, softly blowing on them.

We sat around the fire on our blankets, taking in the magical beauty of this night. "This is the greatest," Allison commented. "I haven't done anything like this in ages."

"I've always felt very connected with the sea," said Elinor.

"Being here with the moon is especially perfect. You can't get much more feminine than this."

"I have a friend," said Lena, "who went to Brazil a few years back. They have a huge ceremony there on New Year's Eve for the Goddess of the Sea—Yemanja. She is also similar to the Virgin Mary—the ultimate compassionate mother. Over a million people in Rio de Janeiro go down to the ocean each year to make offerings to this goddess. It's part of a religious tradition that originally came from the slaves who were brought to Brazil from West Africa. She showed me pictures of another ceremony to Yemanja where the women wore long, full, blue colored skirts. She told me they do special dances and sing songs to Yemanja, swaying their skirts to imitate the motion of waves."

"That sounds beautiful," said Alex, longingly. "I would love to be part of something like that."

"You can!" Sophie exclaimed. "Let's go down by the water. Come on girls." She took off her shoes, jumped up and headed down toward the water. Several of us followed.

As we got closer to the surf line, we could feel the huge power of the ocean. Sophie grabbed my hand and started running down the beach. One by one we linked hands and in a serpentine line ran down the beach, dashing in and out of the water, weaving back and forth. "This is too good for them to miss," Lena cried, looking back at the rest of the women huddled around the fire. "Let's go get them."

We ran up to the fire and grabbed the others, ignoring a few weak protests. Sophie led us back down to the surf. The waves crashed around our feet, drenching us from the knees down, but nobody seemed to care. Exhilarated, we danced around, shrieking wildly. Allison waded into the water and, lifting her arms high, began to spin around.

Lena began yelling, "Las Chicas Locas, Las Chicas Locas!" as she ran through the white sea foam, with her skirt lifted up to her hips.

"Crazy girls, crazy girls," cried Allison in response, laughing as she grabbed Lena's hand, and they danced an impromptu jig at the edge of the surf.

We collapsed in a wet, salty heap on the sand, giggling breathlessly. "That was so fun," exclaimed Allison.

"I wish some of my 'old lady' friends could see me now," chuckled Elinor.

"You don't seem any the worse for wear," I noticed.

"Actually, I feel quite revived. We should do this more often," she agreed.

With sparkling eyes and rosy cheeks, we traipsed back to the fire to dry off and have some refreshments.

"When we were dancing in the waves, I felt like a goddess for a moment," said Sylvia, breathlessly. "I've never felt anything like that before. I was expanded, huge. All this energy was running through me. Even now I can feel my fingertips tingling. It was a very different me than the person who goes to the office everyday."

"I feel that up on my land in the hills sometimes," said Sophie. "There are nights during the summer when the Santa Ana winds blow—the hot winds. They make me feel wild. I go out on the deck and lift up my arms, feeling the wind on my body. I start to feel like I'm a part of the wind. I pretend I'm a bird—a hawk riding the thermal currents." She stopped, looking out at the moon, which, by now, was high over the silver sea. We sat quietly for a while, watching the fire and listening to the waves.

Creating a Relationship with the Archetypal Feminine

Toward the end of our evening at the beach, we decided to each bring some object to the next group that we felt symbolized something about our sacred femininity. The following week, we arrived with various bundles in hand. We peeked jokingly at each other's stuff as we sat down and began the meeting. Lena placed a woven cloth, another of her treasures from Mexico, in the middle of the circle. One by one we went around the circle, sharing something about the significance of what we brought with us.

"Well, I'll go first," said Sophie. "I know this may seem weird, but I had such a strong impulse to do this." She placed a paintbrush and a palette knife on the cloth. "I kept thinking I should bring something pretty and feminine. But, for me, my painting tools are a bridge to the sacred part of myself. When I paint, I feel most alive and most aligned with God. After our last conversation about this, when I painted, I started imagining that I was some kind of creation goddess, bringing things into life with my brush."

"Could you paint me as some kind of skinny girl next?" joked Lena, "I'll try anything." She unwrapped an object from some cloth and showed it to the group. It was a two-headed ceramic female figure. "I found this figurine in Mexico, in an art studio along side the road. A lot of the stuff we saw down there was pretty schlocky, but this one was different. I like her because she symbolizes my feminine spirit that has more than one face. There's the one that I show to the world, and another one that looks in a very different direction."

Jenny opened the cardboard box that was by her feet. Carefully, unwrapping the tissue paper that protected it, she unrolled a good-sized discarded snakeskin and put it on the blanket.

"Wow," said Allison. "Creepy! Where did you get that?"

"I found it one day a while ago when I was out for a walk," answered Jenny. "It was completely intact. There was no sign of the snake that left it, thank goodness. I didn't really know what to do with it until we were asked to do this exercise, and it seemed like the perfect thing. Lately I feel a lot like a creature that has shed their skin. My life is going through so many changes. I guess if there's a goddess of transformation, I hope she's looking down on me."

"I brought my dancing shoes," declared Elinor, putting a pair of Capezio ballroom dancing shoes on the blanket. "They symbolize the part of me that loves to dance, that, I hope, will never stop dancing. I just started going back to ballroom dancing classes. I'd stopped after my husband died. But I'm really glad I'm doing it again. It makes me feel very alive. I think that one part of my sacred femininity is a dancing goddess."

"I brought this conch shell that I found skin diving in Jamaica," I said, showing them a large conch with a deep orange and rose-colored interior. "It seems very organically female to me, almost sexual. When I look at it, I see the beauty of my feminine sensuality. There's also the sense that some of it is mysteriously hidden in the inside of the spiral."

Allison shyly showed us a photograph of herself. It showed her kneeling naked gracefully on a rock staring into a pool of green water. Her long blonde hair had fallen forward, and had caught the sunlight. "Billy took this picture of me on a camping trip. He encouraged me to bring it. He says I look like some kind of fairy or nature sprite."

"It's beautiful, Allison," exclaimed Elinor. "You do look absolutely magical."

"I couldn't decide what to bring," said Alex. "I feel like there are so many parts of me vying for attention right now. But I finally settled on a picture of Michelangelo's *Pieta*." She had an art book opened to a photograph of the famous sculpture. "I've always really loved this piece. Her face is so full of love as she holds the dead Christ on her lap. I want to be able to bring that kind of compassion to my kids."

Everyone had taken a turn except Sylvia. She looked distressed as she said, "This was hard for me. I couldn't think of anything. I don't feel particularly feminine, and some of this goddess stuff makes me uncomfortable. I was raised in a devout Christian household and some of what we've been talking about would make my parents' hair stand on end. It goes against the beliefs I was raised with. But I found this book at the library that talks about Sophia as the feminine side of God. She is supposed to be the embodiment of God's wisdom. I like that, because I would love to feel wise. And to me, books are symbols of wisdom." She carefully placed the book next to Allison's self-portrait.

We spent some time reflecting on and examining the different images that now colorfully filled the center of the circle. Seeing them all together was like beholding a visual mandala of the many faces of the archetypal feminine.

Fierce Beauty Tip

Gather a variety of objects that symbolically convey your sacred feminine. Find a special place in your home or your yard. Spread out a piece of fabric and arrange the objects upon it with care and reverence. Honoring these objects is honoring you. You may want to make this "altar" a permanent part of your home.

Communing with Archetypes

There are different kinds of relationships that we can have with archetypes. Most women will find that they already have a strong connection with a particular archetype. Or more accurately, an archetypal pattern or energy may have made a claim on you. Sometimes we may even have more than one voice clamoring for our attention. The archetypal patterns that influence us may also change during the course of our lives. At any given time, however, there is usually one predominant voice in our psyche.

The archetypal forces that influence us are, for the most part, gifts to be enjoyed, but they need to be kept in balance. For example, I have, for many years, been what the African Yoruba call a "child of Oshun." Oshun is much like the Greek goddess Aphrodite. She is sensual, romantic, and loves beautiful clothes and jewelry as well as music and dance. She is a lover and wants endlessly to be in love, to be courted and to be the object of men's admiration and desire. This is all great except for the fact that Oshun doesn't know beans about the realities of sustaining long-term, enduring partnerships and marriages. That's really not her thing. She just wants to play.

When I got married, it was necessary for me to let her know that there were certain boundaries that she had to respect. I needed this elemental force, which could be my creative genius, to take a bit of a back seat, so as not to be my downfall. I needed this part of me to find a balance with the other human needs that I had for companionship, stability and deep intimacy. The light side, or light mirror, of the Oshun/Aphrodite archetype has a wonderful feminine *joie de vivre*—a capacity to take great pleasure and enjoyment in life—as well as an earthy sensuality. The dark mirror of this archetype is expressed in a woman who is obsessed with relationships, who loses herself in her need for attention from others, and needs constantly to be adored.

Fierce Beauty Tip

Through doing the previous exercises as well as exploring the mythological stories of other cultures, identify the feminine archetype that you feel intuitively most connected with. Make a list of her helpful and unhelpful qualities. Write a letter thanking her for her gifts and expressing the boundaries that you would like her to respect.

Another type of connection with an archetype comes about through conscious intention. You may have a need in your life, a lack of a certain kind of energy, or an inadequately developed capability. You may want to conceive a child, or be a better mother. You may want to get in touch with your sensuality. You may be uncomfortable with asserting and standing up for yourself and need to build rapport with a feminine power goddess. In this case, it is useful to search out information about different kinds of archetypes that can help you to develop and strengthen other parts of your being.

Communing with archetypes is much like conversing with deceased loved ones. We speak with them and feel their presence in our minds and hearts. In these moments we are using the technique of active imagination, because we are actively engaging with their image as if we are talking to an actual physical person

In the Fierce Beauty Club, our work with archetypes started out more like "let's pretend." We then began to develop into real relationships with these old voices sleeping in the emerald-green pool of the female psyche. The various exercises and art projects that we did were tantamount to sweeping the floor, filling a vase with fresh flowers and putting a welcome mat outside our door in preparation for a welcome guest.

Whole Goddesses: Embracing Our Light and Dark Sides

In our next few meetings the Fierce Beauties brought in images and stories of goddesses and feminine characters from myths and fairy tales. Because the field of goddess mythology was so large, we decided to narrow our focus by creating categories of goddesses that we were most interested in exploring. We were deeply moved by these bigger-than-life mythological women who exemplified aspects of femininity that eluded us in our ordinary lives.

One of our first discoveries was the large number of goddess figures who possessed traits that, from a Western perspective, were paradoxical. Our culture's moral and religious structures usually divide human behavior into dualistic polarities of good and evil. There are other spiritual systems, however, in which what is considered sacred, or holy, is more inclusive.

For example, the ancient Sumerian goddess Inanna's realm spanned all the universe from the heavens, where she is associated with the planet Venus, to the earth in her capacity of goddess of fertility, and to the underworld. She is the goddess of love and war, as well as of gentle rains and violent, turbulent storms. She is the embodiment of the full potency of feminine energy in all its many forms. In one of her hymns, Inanna tells a story about Enki, the Sumerian god of wisdom, who gives her the "me," the holy laws of heaven and earth:

> *He gave me the art of the hero*
> *He gave me the art of power*
> *He gave me the art of treachery*
> *He gave me the art of straightforwardness*
> *He gave me the plundering of cities*
> *He gave me the setting up of lamentations*
> *He gave me the rejoicing of the land.*

Enki gave her many powers that would not be considered good or holy in the moral structure of our culture. The dualistic worldview is not present in Sumerian cosmology, particularly not in the myth of Inanna. She is a lusty, passionate goddess who is also a wise ruler, lawmaker and warrior. She nurtures life, procreates and then destroys with equal passion and abandon. She is wild, uninhibited and untamed—the queen of Heaven and Earth.

Another example of a "whole goddess" is the Egyptian deity, Isis, whose reign as one of the most significant figures in the Egyptian pantheon extended over 700 years, from the third century B.C.E. past the fourth century C.E. She was worshipped widely throughout the ancient classical world. Isis was considered to be the primary creator of the universe. Known as the "One Who Is All," "Giver of Life" and "Lady of the House of

Life," her vast realm extended beyond the earth into the after-world, where she bestowed eternal life on her loyal subjects. She gave birth to the sun and caused the movements of heavenly bodies. The Nile River arose from the tears she shed because of the death of her husband, Osiris. In one of her hymns, reminiscent of Inanna, she proclaims:

> *I gave and ordained the laws of men, which no one*
> *is able to change . . .*
> *I am she that is called goddess by women . . .*
> *I divided the earth from the heaven.*
> *I ordered the paths of stars . . .*
> *I made strong the right*
> *I brought together women and men . . .*
> *I am the Queen of wars.*
> *I am the Queen of the thunderbolt.*
> *I stir up the sea and I calm it.*
> *I am in the rays of the sun*
> *I set free those in bonds*
> *I overcome Fate.*

The most famous story about Isis recounts the death and dismemberment of Osiris at the hands of his dark brother Set. Isis searches for the pieces of his body, reassembles them and returns him to life. He is complete with the exception of his missing penis, which Isis then creates out of clay. In her darker aspect, she is Nephthys, the "Crone of Death," who destroys life. She was finally absorbed, like many other female deities worldwide, into the Christian mother goddess, Mary.

Some women tell me that when they encounter these diverse images, they often feel a sense of relief. Most of us instinctively know that we are a mixture of many light and dark qualities. Many of us, however, have attempted futilely to repress those parts of ourselves that we believe are inappropriate or that our culture finds unacceptable. When we look into the mirror of the archetypal feminine, we find the whole of ourselves reflected back—without apology or excuse. Stories and myths that describe "whole goddesses" give women the inspiration to love *all* their parts.

Fierce Beauty Tip

Find a whole goddess with whom you feel connected. Make a list of the parts of yourself that you judge critically and reimagine them as sacred qualities. Notice how many different aspects of your psyche, light and dark, are reflected in the mirror of the whole goddess.

Wild Goddesses: Reclaiming Your Untamed Self

Because we live in houses with artificial lighting, have minimal contact with the elemental world and, to some degree, have lost an awareness of the internal rhythms of the animal body, we are in great danger of losing our wildness. The archetype of the wild goddess, like many rare species, is almost in danger of extinction in our imagination. Mary Oliver makes a plea for the return of the wild goddess when she writes in her poem *Wild Geese*, "You only have to let the soft animal of your body love what it loves." The wild goddesses return us to a place of instinctive knowing. They can bring a balance to the human psyche that has lost much of its inherent body wisdom through hundreds of years of Western logos, science and technology.

Clarissa Pinkola Estés, who wrote the seminal work on this archetype, *Women Who Run With the Wolves*, says that without the Wild Woman, "women lose touch with their soulfooting. Without her, they forget why they're here. . . . Without her they are silent when they are in fact on fire. The Wild Woman is their regulator, she is their heart."

The wild goddess is most at home in nature, away from the complex, heady pace of urban life. Her friends are oceans, rivers, plants, trees, wild beasts and birds. In Western culture we know her as Diana, or Artemis, who was the goddess of wild lands and hunting for many centuries throughout the classical world. The people of India call their wild goddesses *yakshis*. They are found in countless murals, friezes and sculptures, intertwined with vines and flowers, animals and snakes. In Hawaii, the wild goddess is Pele's sister Hi'iaka, whose home is in the sacred groves of the flowering 'ohia-lehua trees and ferns. There, reluctant ever to leave, she dances with the forest spirits.

In Dr. Estés story "La Loba," she tells us that La Loba, the Wolf Woman, prowls the desert arroyos of the Southwest, collecting bones. She wanders the hot desert looking for wolf bones, which she brings back to her cave. There, before the fire, she carefully arranges the bones and begins to sing over them with a low, wailing chant. Gradually as she croons, the bones grow flesh, muscle develops, hair grows. La Loba leans low, singing and breathing life into the wolf. The wolf takes a breath, opens her eyes, leaps up and lopes off into the night. Some people report that they've seen the wolf change into a laughing woman in the moonlight.

Have we been away too long from our natural home? The responsibilities we carry for the people we love, the burdens of financial survival and the distractions of modern life conspire to separate us from our wildness. If you feel like your vitality is low and your thinking confused, perhaps you have been too long away from the true home of your wild soul.

Many years ago, there was a terrible storm that wreaked havoc upon my home in Northern California. Fierce winds and rain caused a number of tall Douglas fir trees to fall, like pick-up sticks, on the house, the outbuildings and the land. They upended, leaving huge craters in the earth. It rained nonstop for days. We lived without electricity or running water, in the midst of this utter destruction, for four days. One day, my friend Helen, arrived and insisted on taking me out to walk in the storm.

She lived on 80 acres of meadows and redwood forest. We walked in the pouring rain with our slickers and rubber boots. For the first time, I felt the beauty of this wild tropical storm. I could feel the warm, moist air and the steady rain penetrating the soil. The forest and the fields seemed to be thoroughly enjoying themselves, oblivious to the human concerns that so plagued me. I felt, for the first time in days, that I was a part of the wild, elemental movements that surrounded me, rather than at war with them. In that moment I was communing with the wild goddess. I understood that the destruction around me was part of nature recreating herself.

☀ Fierce Beauty Tip

Go hunting for the wild goddess. She can be found in wild, passionate music or the elemental forces of nature. Relax your mind, let go of your everyday cares for a little while and surrender to a deeper dance. Feel your body and soul expand, becoming a part of the pulsing web of life.

Erotic Goddesses: Owning Our Passions

The archetype of the erotic goddess has left a trail of flower petals across the world. She is the personification of love, joy, sensuality and pleasure. She is a wonderful source of support and inspiration for women who feel disenfranchised from their feminine sensuality, or who have lost connection with their capacity to experience joy and pleasure. In our culture, the media has heavily defined, exploited and co-opted this archetype, manipulating images of beautiful women for commercial and entertainment purposes. As a result, many women believe that goddesses of Eros, such as the Greek Aphrodite, are only available to women who possess a particular, socially sanctioned form of beauty.

The erotic goddesses are not evoked by fear-inspired obsessions with our appearance. Instead, they enter our lives on the wings of joy and the sounds of laughter. We can evoke Aphrodite through following the beckoning of our sensual pleasures. She loves to eat, dance, sing, make love and decorate herself. She loves all forms of art, but is most present in the fullness of our open hearts. One of Aphrodite's representatives was Marilyn Monroe, not simply because of her physical beauty, but also because of her tremendous capacity for sensuality and joy. Like her African sister, Oshun, Aphrodite is associated with the sun, because of her association with goldenness and "life-infusing warmth." Her heat and passion bring about all acts of creation. It is Aphrodite who inspires attraction and sexuality.

Xochuiqetzal is the Aztec goddess of flowers, singing, dancing and love. Full of life and gaiety, she lives on a mountaintop surrounded by musicians and dancers. She is named the "Goddess of All Women." She is the special patron of all lovers and courtesans. Xochuiqetzal brought language to her people through her sacred messenger, the dove.

The Haitian goddess of love and sensuality is Erzulie. Filmmaker Maya Deren, in her book *The Divine Horseman*, describes Erzulie: "As Lady of Luxury she gives gifts constantly . . . she is, above all, Goddess of Love, that human luxury of the heart. . . . She is as lavish with that love as she is generous with her gifts. In ceremonies, when Erzulie graces her devotees with her presence, she first carefully washes, then grooms and adorns herself. She is the essence of feminine sensuality."

If you need more playfulness, romance and sensuality in your life, it is helpful to create a relationship with a goddess of love. If your natural connection with your sexuality has been disturbed through some form of abuse or repressive conditioning, then the erotic goddess can help restore what is your divine birthright—to fully enjoy your female body and express your sexuality. If you fear that doing this will bind you in unhealthy ways to men and male fantasies, the erotic goddess will guide you in creating ownership and command of this domain. The love goddess also assists women in discovering a more fulfilling connection with a deeper, more available source of beauty.

At one of the first women's conferences I ever attended, many years ago, I had the rare pleasure of witnessing a dance performance, called "The Vulva Dance" by a woman named Arisika Razak. A tall, ample African-American woman, she entered the stage wrapped in flowing, white material arranged fluidly and casually over her body. To the sound of slow, rhythmic music, she began to undulate her hips and move gracefully around the room. As the music continued almost hypnotically, she slowly removed the fabric draped over her body, and emerged entirely naked. As she swayed gently, knees bent, head tilted, she held her hands and fingers together over her belly in a triangular position to represent the sacred female vulva. Her unabashed, sensual and unhidden presence deeply moved me. I knew that I was witnessing the immanence of the erotic goddess.

☀ Fierce Beauty Tip

Take an oil-scented bath by candlelight. Scatter flowers petals into the queen's bath. When you are finished, dry yourself off with soft towels and rub your body with fragrant lotions. Dress yourself in the most sensual fabrics you can find in your closet. Notice the way they feel and move against your skin. Welcome the erotic goddess that is you!

Power Goddesses: Accessing Our Inner Authority

Despite all that women have learned collectively in the last 30 years, many of us still muddle somewhat ineffectively through our lives, at the mercy of situations and relationships that may not serve us well. Vital strength, focus, assertiveness and the capacity to think and act strategically often seem to elude us. Connecting with power goddesses can assist us in accessing these qualities.

Power goddesses are often associated with the element of fire. Female deities connected with the sun, such as Egyptian Sekhmet, Japanese Amaterasu and Roman Sulis Minerva, embody this archetype. The Egyptian goddess Sekhmet is one of the most powerfully evocative images of the sun goddess. The daughter of Ra, the sun god, she is called the "Eye of Ra." Represented in statues as a lion-headed goddess, she was "adopted by the pharaohs as a symbol of their own unvanquishable heroism in battle . . . she breathes fire against the king's enemies." She is known to be extremely fierce and violent, but is also associated with the healing arts and is called the "Lady of Life." She is often depicted holding an ankh, the Egyptian symbol of life. Sekhmet is also called "the Mighty One" and regarded as one "great of magic."

Through communing with this archetype, women can access their authority and assert their individuality. Sekhmet's power can give us the necessary courage and will to move out of victimization and codependency. She can enable women to be aggressive, when necessary, protecting fiercely their own boundaries and the well-being of their families. The archetype of the sun helps women to enhance their ability to be consistent, to hold intention and to be goal-oriented. Sun power can help us move beyond our biology into a place of willful action. For women, this is often the strength needed to move beyond the traditional roles of mother and wife, and establish careers in the outer world.

The Hawaiian goddess Pele is an archetypal force whose power comes from the fire in the center of the earth. Pele is the burning core that inexorably and willfully moves up and out, destroying the old land and giving birth to the new almost simultaneously. Her sacred name, *Ka-ula-o-ke-ahi*, means the "redness of the fire." In stories she can change her shape at will, sometimes appearing as an ancient hag and other times as a beautiful young woman. When she's angry, which happens frequently, she appears cloaked in flames.

Pele represents the force of our righteous anger, which cleans away the old debris of life patterns that no longer serve us, and makes way for new growth. She is the fire in the center of our soul, which activates when the pressure builds too high. Known also as "the eater of the land," Pele's domain is the transformation of our psyche. Like other power goddesses, Pele can injure and destroy what gets in her path. She is a force to be reckoned with and taken very seriously. Ultimately, her power is in the service of our souls, but she can wreak havoc in the process.

Other power goddesses are also associated with extreme weather conditions in nature. The West African deity Oya, is a goddess of sudden change. A potent warrioress, she is connected with tornados, whirlwinds, lightning and thunder. She carries a sword in each hand and battles all that she perceives as unjust. Yoruba priestess Luisah Teish writes: "Oya doesn't just rearrange the furniture in the house—She knocks the building to the ground."

Oya has the energy to significantly transform our lives, but she can also be destructive. If you are experiencing too much change, if things are happening too fast, you may want to respectfully ask this archetypal energy to back off a bit. If your life seems to be in constant upheaval, with frequent changes in relationships, jobs and living situations, if you are volatile and often find yourself enraged for no legitimate reason, Oya or Pele may be out of balance in your psyche.

There are many other power goddesses found in mythology. Often little understood by Western researchers, their domains are often paradoxically concerned with death and life. Their symbols can be gruesome, like those of the Aztec goddess

Coatlicue, also called the "Lady of the Serpent Skirt," who wore a necklace of skulls and a skirt of snakes. Like Pele, she was also a maker of volcanoes. The Hindu goddess, Kali, deeply revered in India, is both the creatrix of life as well as a bloodthirsty destroyer. These archetypes teach us about the fundamental interdependency of life and death. They reflect an understanding of the cyclic nature of life, in which life and death give birth to one another in an endless circle.

☀Fierce Beauty Tip

To learn how to defend your boundaries; do a visualization in which you imagine yourself as a great warrioress. You wear a special suit of power, and in your hand is a sword. See yourself standing at the threshold of your domain, ready to protect the sovereign, sacred and precious being that you are. See yourself fiercely and firmly fending off the people in your life who attempt to cross your boundaries without your permission.

Mother Goddesses: Connecting with Our Compassionate Hearts

The mother goddess is perhaps the most well known and accessible of female archetypes. Present all over the world at various times, she is still worshipped widely in the Catholic Church as the Virgin Mary and the Virgin of Guadalupe. In China, she is known as Kwan Yin, the "Lady Who Brings Children." In Japan, she is Kwannon, Mother of Compassion. Sometimes the mother goddesses are associated with the boundless fertility and fecundity of the earth, as is the case with the Hopi Indian Corn Mother, who ensures that her people will have sufficient food, and the Greek goddess Demeter. Other mother goddesses are symbolically connected with the boundless, deep ocean, such as the Brazilian goddess Yemanja.

Many of the earliest archeological finds are ancient female

figurines, such as the Venus of Willendorf, giving rise to the widespread belief that primitive humanity worshipped the sacred mother. These goddesses are often very wide-hipped and big-bottomed, with huge, pendulous breasts. They are images of earthy women who know how to sustain the lives of babies, families and whole communities. Archeologists, such as Marija Gimbutas, found evidence that early men and women regarded women's capacity to procreate as divine and utterly magical. This profound act of creation was symbolized by menstrual blood. The Great Mother is said to have "not only created the world out of her interior ocean of blood; she kept the gods alive with periodic infusions of this magic elixir."

There are many reasons to create a personal connection with a mother goddess. If you have been inadequately mothered as a child, the mother goddess can fill some of those empty holes that are so difficult heal. She can be a source of comfort and safety, a place to tend the small and vulnerable places in us. In this capacity, I think of her as the "Great Heart of the World."

If you are currently a mother and feel that your resources are inadequate, the mother goddess stands behind you, feeding you, as you feed others. If you lack the necessary patience and tenderness that those in your care require, connecting with a mother goddess can inspire and educate you. If you feel stretched thin between the demands of work and family, unable to give everyone what they need, the mother goddess can help you to access nurturing strength and perseverance. As women, we so often feel alone in our responsibilities. Connecting with this archetype places us in a lineage of mothers, the Mother-line, with its vast repository of information about conceiving, birthing, nursing, mothering, aging, grandmothering and dying.

The mother goddess is also known as Gaia, the living body of our planet, the earth. She is the ground beneath us, holding us firmly in her gravitational field. This aspect of the Great Mother can help restore our balance if we have lost our sense of being rooted in our own bodies. Losing the ground can happen for many reasons. We may be living a manic lifestyle, moving rapidly through space and time, binging on experience without digesting it properly. We may have come to distrust our body, if we have suffered physical harm or illness. If you have chronic pain of any kind, you may be disconnected from your body. We may simply be avoiding being completely present and embodied for fear of being completely alive. In any case, being centered and rooted in the physical body is a place of power for women.

We can reconnect with the earth mother through putting our hands in the dirt and creating a garden or getting some kind of nurturing bodywork. I didn't completely inhabit my body until I was about 30 years old and had my first massage. Before that I was often tired and cold, with a weak immune system. When I got massaged, however, my body felt absolutely safe and comfortable, for perhaps the first time in my life. At a very deep level of my psyche something changed. I decided that this business of living in a human body was all right, maybe even enjoyable.

☀Fierce Beauty Tip

If you find yourself in need of comfort and nurturing, imagine that you are sitting in the lap of a large woman. You are completely at home here. This is where you belong. Allow yourself to completely relax, knowing that in this moment, you are held and protected by the Great Mother. Feel the warmth of her heart, the softness of her breast and the peace emanating from her soul.

Wise Goddesses: Making Important Choices

The archetype of the wise goddess offers women spiritual and intellectual guidance as they negotiate the complexities of human existence. Often depicted in mythology as an elder woman or crone, the wise goddess is a seer, a prophesier. She has a deeper and more far-reaching perspective, born in part, from the experience gained from her advanced years, and in part from her proximity to her own death. The wise goddess is partially "between the worlds." She has moved through the seasons of life and approaches her return to a different realm. Therefore, she can often see and perceive information that is not available to those of us who are still engaged actively in the fullness of life.

The term hag, a somewhat derogatory word used to describe old women, comes from the Greek word *hagia*, which means "holy one." Some researchers believe that in many of the pre-Christian matriarchal tribal cultures, it was the elder women who were the first lawmakers. In very early Egypt, the elder women were in charge of the *hekau*, which were the sacred "words of power." The Egyptian goddess Hekat takes her name from the word *hek*, which means intelligence.

The Greek goddess Hecate, is a later offshoot of this same wise goddess archetype. Hecate's domain is the underworld and all things related to magic and prophesy. She was worshipped at many crossroads in her function as intermediary between one world and the other. In the middle ages, like many elder women, Hecate became personified in a more negative way. Instead of being regarded as a holy sage, she was feared as a dark and malevolent witch.

In Navaho mythology, the wise goddess is called Spider Woman or Grandmother Spider. She is the "Spinner of the threads of fate or destiny." Spider Woman is small and unobtrusive, yet powerful. Her voice is difficult to hear, we may have to listen carefully. In the Navaho creation myth, she says, "Only those who forget why they came into this world will lose their way." Her function is to restore us to the center of the web. Spider Woman helps us hold the thread of existence. She helps us to remember our deep purpose, the deep song of the soul.

In the early Gnostic versions of the bible, which were not canonized into law, the feminine face of god was known as Sophia, the Goddess of Wisdom. There are frequent references to Sophia, whose name means wisdom, as working in partnership with God to create the world. Some believe that Sophia was originally the Holy Ghost. She is still worshipped as St. Sophia in the Greek Orthodox Church, and a shrine was built for her in the sixth century, known as the Church of Hagia Sophia.

Sophia reappears in the Jewish cabalistic texts as the Shekinah, the soul of god. The Jewish cabalist mystics believe that it is essential to reunite the masculine and feminine aspects of God. The Shekinah derives from the Hindu Shakti, also known as the feminine soul of god. The Hindus believe that God cannot act without Shakti, it is through her that the spark of life comes into being.

A good time to consult the wise goddess is when you are at a crossroads in your life. There are times in our relationships or careers when significant life choices must be made, with long-ranging consequences. At times like this, we may not be able to make decisions without tuning into a deeper intuitive compass that aligns us with our destiny. Spider Woman or Hecate can bring us the insight that we need to walk with sure feet. Their wisdom comes from stepping out and away from the details of everyday life and tuning in to the bigger picture.

If you are a woman approaching later life, the wise goddess is knocking on your door. She is calling on you to take your place as a female elder who speaks the words of power that our communities need to hear. The wise goddess, the sacred holy hag, does not feel invisible or irrelevant to the people around her. She knows who she is and the gifts she has to give. Whatever you may have learned throughout your long life, there is some person who needs to receive that learning.

Living Goddesses: Claiming Our Sacredness

For several months the Fierce Beauty Club immersed ourselves in goddess lore from cultures around the world. It was an exciting adventure with lots of aha's and connections being made.

"When Liz first told us about the Motherline," said Allison, "I didn't have a very clear idea about what she meant. It was abstract to me. But now, after learning about the goddesses, I understand it better. I can *feel* generations of women passing down their wisdom. I can imagine their faces and see them sitting around fires in caves wearing skins."

"To me, learning about the sacred feminine has been like eating a wonderful feast," pronounced Lena. "All these images of powerful women are like an array of beautiful fruits and flowers. I feel pleasantly well fed."

"What about you, Sylvia?" I asked.

"Well, I started out reading about Sophia, but that was pretty heady stuff," Sylvia responded. "There's a big debate about her role in the scriptures. But I felt very drawn to the wild goddesses. My name actually comes from the Latin name for forest. It seems appropriate. There's a whole different me that comes alive when I'm out in the woods. I feel like a wild spirit. I fit in better in the forest than I do elsewhere. My size seems right instead of being too big. I'm strong and I like to use my body."

"It was very helpful to me to hear about the wise crone goddesses," Elinor jumped in. "At my age, it's so easy to think that you have no real function left in the world. I got so inspired that I joined a group of volunteer senior citizens that helps small businesses get off the ground."

"I love the erotic goddesses," gushed Lena. "I'm completely at home in that arena. I really do feel like I'm in a lineage."

"Well, you *would*," replied Alex, laughing playfully at Lena. "We know what you've got on your mind."

"I especially like the power goddesses," announced Jenny. "I'm imagining myself like Pele, cloaked in flames. Since my life is in a state of total upheaval, I like to think that my rage is creating new land out of the ashes."

The world of the sacred feminine has a great deal to offer women. It can give us a frame of reference for what we already know about ourselves, as well as opening up new possibilities. The feminine archetypes are boundless repositories of knowledge about the complex and diverse nature of femininity. Sometimes, we must be like La Loba, the Wolf Woman who sings over the bones of the dead wolf, restoring life to her. We can sing over the bones of forgotten and misplaced bones of the feminine soul, breathing new life and vitality into ourselves and other women whose lives we touch.

Fierce Beauty Tip

Get together with a girlfriend and make masks of your sacred feminine using plaster gauze strips (found at your local craft store). Following the instructions on the package, lay the moistened strips on your partner's face and invite the sacred feminine essence of this woman to reveal herself through the mask. When the mask dries, decorate it as directed by the goddess herself.

✶Fierce Beauty Tip

Get together with your women friends and have a party where you each come dressed as your favorite goddess figure. Celebrate the sacred feminine spirit!

• • •

STEP 3: Embrace the Divine Feminine within you.

CHAPTER 4

Claiming the Lost Parts of Ourselves

To live with shadow awareness is to turn away
from the peaks toward the valleys,
away from the heights and the rarefied air,
toward the depths and the dark.
—Connie Zweig and Steve Wolf

SINCE OUR LAST MEETING Sophie and her husband had built an open fire pit on their land. She invited us to bring some portable lawn chairs with us to the meeting so that we could comfortably sit outside around the fire. As I walked down the path from the studio, I could see that Sophie had already gotten the fire started.

In ones and twos the women arrived and found their spots, trying to stay away from the smoky side of the fire pit.

"This is great," Alex said enthusiastically. "I feel like a little kid on a camping trip. I haven't done anything like this in years."

"It's like we've stepped back in time," commented Sylvia. "We're practically prehistoric."

We spent some time going around the circle and checking in about our lives since we had last seen each other. Jenny, looking pale with dark circles under her eyes, said, "I've just had my period and I got so depressed right before it started. There were a few days when I just cried all the time and felt hopeless about everything."

"That happens to me too sometimes," Allison sympathized.

"Don't you think that women naturally make downward journeys into the unconscious because of our menstrual cycles?" asked Sophie. "I sure feel like I go into a black hole when I'm about to get my period."

"Definitely," I answered. "A friend of mine once said to me, 'You can't be a woman without descending into the underworld.' It's built into our organic biological rhythm. Every month, for many years, a lot of us go through a process of coming apart. There's a wonderful picture in Esther Harding's book, *Woman's Mysteries*, that shows women in different phases of the moon cycle depicted in varying stages of becoming mermaids. The woman in the dark of the moon phase, which, in ancient times, was associated with menstruation, has become a full mermaid, completely immersed in the ocean. The woman at the full moon phase, during ovulation, has emerged completely from the sea."

We move, in the course of a monthly cycle, in and out, back and forth, up and down. Our movement takes us deep into the interior of our soul and then back out again into the day world. At menstruation, we are most focused toward the unconscious, the deep ocean of the soul. In modern times, however, we're not as in touch with our women's cycles. We often attempt to override the body and the soul's need for periodic rejuvenation through decreased external activity and communion with our internal world.

We have a great opportunity, if we can allow the feelings, to use the organic downward momentum to pay attention to our deep parts. In this area, women have an advantage over men in that our bodies take us down regularly, whether we like it or not, providing an opportunity for emotional cleansing.

Maren Hansen, in her book *Mother Mysteries*, writes about nature's abduction of a woman's ego when she becomes pregnant. She is asked to "sacrifice her ego, her sense of individuality, her self-determination, her body, her mind, her feelings." The hormones that are released to create the necessary flexibility in a pregnant woman's physical structure also affect her emotional and psychological makeup, transforming her in preparation for her new responsibility.

When we go through menopause, we again have a powerful hormonally-based opportunity for transformation. The ego structure that forms our personality, as we know it, loosens its grip as strong hormonal changes flood the body. Joan Borysenko, in *Woman's Book of Life,* calls hot flashes, "psychospiritual opportunities" that "burn away the dross of our lives." As we go through "the change," we reinvent ourselves.

Menstruation, pregnancy and menopause all require a kind of versatility and agility within the female psyche and body. We are built for change. The permeable boundaries in the female psyche that are influenced and interwoven with our biology defy definition and control. They do, however, provide us with access to regular, ongoing communication from the furthermost reaches of the deep psyche. Our feelings and symptoms provide us with information about the condition of our souls.

☀Fierce Beauty Tip

Pay attention to the monthly cyclical movements of your body and soul. Record your observations in your Fierce Beauty journal. Notice your energy level, your emotional state, your inward or outward focus, as well as your day and night dreams. Particularly notice what is revealed just before and during your menses.

Diving into the Green Pool

"So this is a good thing?" asked Jenny. "It's hard to imagine that something that feels so lousy could be in any way positive. "Not only that," she went on, "I keep having these lousy dreams about tidal waves. I'm standing on the edge of the beach and I can see a wall of water in the distance. All around me people are running and screaming. I just stand there, sort of paralyzed. I can see my children way up on the hill, and they seem to be safe. The water makes this horrible sucking noise and it pulls at my ankles. In the distance I can see a school of dolphins cavorting in the waves, and I wonder why they are not worried about the tidal wave."

"I also had a strange dream recently. I was in the middle of an earthquake," reported Sylvia. "I was scrambling to get out of a gully that had opened up beneath me. But it just continued to get deeper and deeper. It scared the hell out of me."

"Why are we having these dreams?" asked Jenny.

"It could be that something is trying to get your attention," Elinor suggested. "Being in the group could be stirring up stuff. I have a lot of friends who are holistic health practitioners. They say it is common, if not expected, that when people start getting body work or homeopathy, they start getting worse before they get better—it's called a healing crisis. The body often has suppressed symptoms that need to be expressed for it to get healthier. The same thing can happen with the psyche."

"The intense feelings we have around our periods and our dreams point the direction to where we all need to go," I proposed. "I think our next step should be to explore the parts of ourselves that hold our shadow—the aspects of ourselves that we don't like or may be afraid to face because they are too painful or threatening. In mythology and in our dreams, the Shadow is often imagined as residing in a subterranean underworld, or a deep water realm.

"These shadow aspects of our psyche stay locked away in a dark closet consuming our vitality and creativity, and undermining our well-being. For women, they often represent lost or suppressed aspects of the feminine soul. We cannot successfully restore our feminine souls without addressing the broken places. Would you all like to hear an old story about this?" I asked, as a thermos of hot chocolate made its way around the circle.

"Go for it," called Alex, producing a bag of marshmallows and some long skewers.

"Well, this story is one of my favorites," I began. "It's a wonderful story about female initiation that comes from the Zulu people in Africa.

"Once upon a time, there was a group of teenage girls who lived together in a small village. They hung out together in kind of a clique, just like many of us had to deal with in high school. And, as often happens in adolescence, there was one girl who stood apart, because she was different from the other girls. She also had a necklace that was especially beautiful and inspired envy and jealousy in the other young women. The group of girls decided to play a trick on this young woman.

"First, they secretly buried their own necklaces in the sand. Then they took their nemesis down to the river and told her that they had all thrown their necklaces into the river to appease the river god. She, being of good heart, wanted to do the same and immediately threw her necklace into the river. The other girls then dug up their necklaces, and ran off laughing snidely, leaving her alone and bereft by the side of the river.

"She wandered sadly alongside the river for some time, praying to the river god to restore her necklace. After some time, she heard the voice of the river spirit telling her to dive into a deep pool. She dove deeply in the deep mysterious green pool of water and arrived on a riverbank, where an old woman was sitting. She was a hideous creature with long scraggly gray hair. Her entire body was covered with red sores. As the young woman stood there, paralyzed with fear, the old hag commanded the young woman to lick her sores. Although the girl was frightened and somewhat repulsed, the courage of her compassionate heart gave her strength and she willingly did so.

Then the old woman told her that because of her bravery

she would help the young woman. At that moment, a terrifying demon monster appeared. With a fierce caterwaul and dripping fangs, he attempted to devour the girl. The old woman threw herself in front of the young woman, shielding her from the monster with her body. Frustrated in his attack, the monster returned to his lair. The old hag then gave the young woman an extraordinarily beautiful necklace and sent her back to the village, instructing her to toss a stone back into the pool as she left and to not look back.

"After doing this, the young woman returned to the village. The other young girls were green with envy, as you can imagine. They clustered around her and wanted to know how they too could get a necklace like hers. She told them about the old woman in the pool. They all rushed down to the river, jumped in. But when the old woman asked them to lick her sores, they all refused, sneering and laughing with disgust at this horrible creature. And, guess what happened?"

"The monster got them?" said Allison.

"It sure did. It ate them all right up. No more snotty, mean girls."

"Ha!" Elinor hooted. "I love it."

Going Down to Greet the Shadow

In our culture there is a great fear of the part of healing that may involve deep feelings. We are a society that strives mightily to avoid pain at any cost. As women enter the workforce and spend more time in a predominantly male culture, there is even more pressure to override "negative" feelings and to disown our ugly, unacceptable parts. We do not want to be seen as weak or emotional. There is little time anymore for inward contemplation or energy available for delving into deep "mysterious green pools."

Consequently, we've lost our bearings when it comes to negotiating our way through the more hidden realms of our being. There are, however, many maps to the underworld still imbedded in mythology and fairy tales. A ubiquitous theme in folk tales all over the world is confrontation with the shadow through descending into the underworld and successfully meeting the challenge of, or defeating, some horrific, monstrous character. These stories hold clues to the importance of making these kinds of explorations, and shed light on the skills needed to achieve a positive outcome. They describe a process of initiation—of transformation from one state of being to another.

The first step in making an underworld journey is to become aware of the beckoning—the downward pull toward the soul and the unconscious. One of the oldest women's initiatory myths comes from the clay Sumerian cuneiform tablets that chronicle the story of the goddess Inanna's descent to the underworld. It opens with:

> "From the Great Above the goddess opened her
>   ear to the Great Below.
> From the Great Above Inanna opened her ear to
>   the Great Below.
> My Lady abandoned heaven and earth to descend
>   to the underworld."

In this myth, the heroine willingly and consciously decides to go down to the underworld. Similarly, in our African story, the young woman hears the call of the river god and chooses to dive into the depths of the unknown. In most versions of the Greek myth of Demeter and Persephone, Persephone is abducted and taken forcibly down into the underworld by Hades. In an older, pre-Hellenic rendition of the myth, however, Persephone hears the wailing voices of the souls caught in the underworld. Out of compassion, she travels to the realm of death to respond to their pleas for assistance.

How do we hear our own call to make this descent in our lives? Sometimes, our choice is made unavoidable through some kind of trauma, either physical or emotional. We may have a car accident, experience a life-threatening or life-changing disease, suffer the loss of a relationship or a significant person. Or we may have some kind of physical or emotional symptoms that indicate a disturbance in our deep psyche that is trying to get our attention.

We can go willingly to the underworld when we make time for reflection and surrender to our feelings. Many of us have a great deal of fear of allowing this kind of loss of control. These kinds of events may plunge us into despair. We may become unglued and undone, feeling like we're falling apart. We don't always know where it will lead us and what the end result will be. Over the years of working with women, however, I've repeatedly seen the rich harvest for those who have the courage and the commitment to make this healing exploration.

Fierce Beauty Tip

Several times a week, take some time away from your life to tune into and reflect on the state of your soul. In a quiet and peaceful spot, allow the cares of daily life to slip away. Listen to what the deeper places have to say. Allow yourself to feel. Tend to what may be untended.

In the story of Inanna's descent, she goes through seven gateways into the underworld. At each gateway, she must relinquish another piece of her royal regalia. As she descends deeper and deeper, she loses the mask with which she meets the day world. She loses her coping skills, her ego structure and her identity, as she knows it. When she reaches the underworld, she is "naked and bowed low." When we dive into the deep pool of our underworld, we sacrifice much of our known ground, and surrender to something deep within us that takes us apart and then rebuilds us anew.

"I know from underworld journeys," said Elinor. "When I had my accident five years ago and broke my back, I went through hell. I was in a great deal of physical pain, but worse than that, I was an emotional wreck. I thought my life was over. I wouldn't be able to walk or dance. I'd be dependent on people. It was very difficult for a long time. There were times when I didn't want to live any more. But my husband and several women friends got me through it, mostly by listening to me and caring. When I look back on that time, it was like being born again."

"I found a great quote in the middle of all this that I pinned up on my wall. It's from Jane Wagner's *The Search for Signs of Intelligent Life in the Universe*. She says "The human mind is kind of like . . . a piñata. When it breaks open, there's a lot of surprises inside. Once you get the piñata perspective, you see that losing your mind can be a peak experience."

We all laughed. It was good to bring some humor into an otherwise heavy topic. It was a part of changing our perspective from fear and avoidance to excitement and expectation. Downward journeys are a part of the natural ecology of the psyche. In nature, forested areas are supposed to burn every so often, as a way of clearing out old debris and making space for new seedlings. If we can understand the necessity of periodic times of falling apart, we can use these experiences as opportunities for tremendous growth.

The Crazy Woman Within

The next step in the mythic process of descending into the underworld is to get to know its inhabitants. After our young Zulu woman dives into the deep pool of water, she arrives on a riverbank where an old woman with sores is sitting. This creature is one version of an archetypal character that shows up frequently in mythology. She is akin to Baba Yaga, the malevolent witch in the Russian fairy tale, who threatens to destroy a young girl named Vasalisa, unless she meets her challenges correctly. In a similar vein, when the goddess Inanna arrives in the underworld, she meets Ereshkigal, who is a raging, old hag-like creature. Confronting the hag within is an essential step of women's initiation into the feminine soul.

Our task is to discover what aspects of our personality have been relegated to the underworld. These are the parts of us that were unacceptable to our parents, our culture, our peers and ultimately to ourselves. They may contain intolerable thoughts or unbearable memories. In most cases they are shrouded in shame. They are often enraged, vengeful, irrational, crazy and chaos-producing. This crazy woman within may be possessed by secret obsessions. Ultimately, she is the part of us that won't toe the party line and rebels against constriction and repression. But her rebellion is often cloaked in a subterfuge of depression, illness, addiction and madness.

In the early versions of the Old Testament of the Bible, it is told that Adam's first wife was named Lilith. Lilith was quite a troublemaker—a fierce beauty in her own right. She refused to make love with Adam on top. Because of her disobedience, she was ejected from the Garden of Eden. She then became a demonic figure who stole children in the night and drove men insane. Similarly, in the fairy tale of Sleeping Beauty, when the thirteenth fairy is not invited to the birthday party of the young princess, she is enraged and casts a spell putting the whole kingdom into an extended sleep.

Wherever the world has disallowed our expression, be it our sexuality, our creative passion, our vulnerabilities or our power, it finds a home in the underworld of our psyche. And often we unknowingly participate by keeping the gates tightly fastened shut, because we are afraid of what might emerge if ever we should relax our hold. There is no keeping the Ereshkigals and the Baba Yagas contained, however. They are simply too devious and too powerful. They will find a way to emerge from the depths. If we commune fearlessly and openly with these unconscious contents, however, we may be able to integrate their vast energy and boundless passion into our beings, instead of becoming possessed and ripped apart by them.

Using active imagination, visualize your personality as a house with many rooms. Explore this house, noticing which rooms are familiar and which are strangers to you. Somewhere in your house is a hidden room, perhaps down in the cellar or up in the attic. Go in search of this room. It contains a part of you that has been lost, disregarded or forgotten.

Ereshkigal Stories

"So, who is the Ereshkigal in each of you?" I queried the group. Despite the crescent moon now high in the sky, the night sky sparkled with a canopy of stars. Sophie heaped more wood on the fire as it began to burn low. "What crazy woman is lurking around in your depths, finding ways to raise a ruckus whenever possible?"

After what seemed like a lengthy pause, Lena spoke up. "Hey, I'll take the plunge. As you all know, I was raised in a devoutly Catholic family and went to a Catholic girl's school as a kid. The Virgin Mary was my first role model. The nuns let us know that sex was a sin and that we should be "good" girls. Well, I wasn't a good girl. I've always been very sexual. I used to masturbate a lot, even when I was only eight or nine years old. I was totally into it. I knew that, according to what I'd been taught, I was doing something really bad, and I would for sure go to hell. I felt incredibly guilty. But the guiltier I felt, the more obsessed I became. It was bizarre.

"As an adult, I feel very conflicted about my sexuality. There's still a part of me that thinks it's wrong and dirty. I tend to attract kind of dangerous men, you know, bad boys. Maybe it's because through them I could act out this "bad girl" part. But those guys usually treat me like shit. Then I react and go to the other end of the spectrum. I get together with a really nice guy and I'm a nice girl. But it's boring. There's hardly any passion. To this day I feel like a bad girl if I enjoy sex. But I still like to masturbate. Are you listening, Sister Mary Francis?" she called out to the ghosts of her past.

We were silent for a bit, thoughtfully taking in what Lena had shared.

Elinor leaned forward and cleared her throat, "I was the child of conservative Methodist parents. My father was very strict and authoritarian. I was the second child, after my sister, who was hell on wheels. She was always in trouble. So I became the good girl who never made any waves. I did what I was told, was very polite and cooperative. My mom used to brag to her friends about what a model child I was. Of course, that didn't do much for my relationship with my sister.

"But it was really a lie, because inside I was seething with resentment. When I got married I continued to try to maintain the facade. I was a good wife and a loving mother. This was during the fifties, when the idealized image of woman was Doris Day in the kitchen with her apron on. I sacrificed my own needs for those of my family. By the time I was 30 I had an ulcer. My rage was eating away at my gut. I've tried to learn, over the years, to let this person out before she becomes a raging maniac, but I'm still working on it."

"That sounds like me," Jenny jumped in, speaking rapidly and breathlessly. "I've really tried to be a good mother to my kids. It's hard to admit this to anyone, but I have moods sometimes when I feel like I hate them. I get cold, dark and withdrawn. When I'm in this space, I don't feel anything except kind of a cold rage. In this state, I can say really mean things to my family that I later regret.

"If I focus on what's going on then, it's almost beyond rage— a kind of hopeless despair and futility. I feel cynical and bitter, and close to giving up sometimes. It's so unlike me to be like that. I love my family. I don't have a clue what to do with all this," she said, twisting her hands anxiously, as her eyes brimmed over with tears.

"Jenny," Alex spoke, looking across the circle at her. "I don't want to take away from what you're feeling, but I think most mothers sometimes just can't stand their kids. I feel that way. It just gets too much, and you lose your marbles. It's a tough thing to admit, though. We're supposed to always be the perfect wives and mothers.

"Something came up for me when we started talking about this stuff. I had a really bad fight with Danny the other day. We're both working incredibly hard right now. There's a lot of pressure. I got so pissed off at him that I hauled off and socked him really hard in the arm. It was late at night and we'd been drinking. It was a bad moment. I felt blown away that I had gotten so out of control. He had quite a bruise in the morning.

"Then I remembered something I hadn't thought of in years. I used to thrash on my younger brother when I was a teenager. Some of it was just roughhousing, but I was bigger than him and could do a lot more damage. It frightens me that I can be violent. What if I lose control with my kids? I would never forgive myself," she said, shaking her head.

The group fell silent again. A few minutes later, the fire made a loud pop, startling us out of our reverie. As I looked around at everyone, I could see a constant interplay of light and shadow on all their faces. A coyote wailed, initiating a round of howling from others in the hills and setting off some of the dogs in nearby houses.

"Part of me is extremely fearful," Sophie began. "I think it's connected with my family history. My grandmother was a holocaust survivor. She made it out of Europe, with my grandfather and my mother, who was just an infant, but many of her family were killed. She suffered terrible poverty as an immigrant in this country. When I was a kid, she used to tell me stories of her husband working in the coal mines in Pennsylvania. He died of black lung disease when he was 45.

"Anyway, I ended up with an extraordinary fear of poverty. I know everyone worries about money, but I sometimes get so panic-stricken that I have trouble breathing. I became an accountant just so that I would know I was in control around money, and yet here I am trying to be an artist. It doesn't make any sense. There's such a large part of me that craves security, yet I want to lead a totally insecure lifestyle. I have to find a way to deal with my fear, though, if I'm going to continue."

"I get very depressed sometimes," Sylvia admitted. "In fact, I'm taking some medication for it." She hesitated and stopped.

"What makes you depressed?" asked Lena.

"Loneliness mostly. I feel very alone in my life. I don't have a partner, and I often feel alienated at work. My time off seems to stretch before me like an empty desert. I'm not very good at reaching out to people. I was an only child and kind of a loner when I went to school. But it wasn't because I wanted to be. I've just always felt so different.

"I can't believe I'm telling you this. I've never admitted it to anyone. But I need friends, and I hate it that I need people. It makes me feel so vulnerable and pitiful. I don't want to need anyone. I just hate this part of me. I wish it would go away," she said vehemently.

"I can relate to hating myself," Allison shared, her long blonde hair covering part of her face. "I've felt like there was something wrong with me my whole life—like I never quite make the grade. I'm not smart enough or pretty enough or pop-ular enough. My mother was always very critical of me, and I guess I've gotten very critical of myself in return. Sometimes I feel like I'm down in a black hole and I can't get out. When I'm in there, there's nothing but badness. I'm not worth any-thing, and everything is my fault. I feel that way when I fight with Billy. It's a horrible feeling."

"Wow," I commented, after she finished. "When we take off the 'everything's cool' mask, there's all this wild stuff going on under the surface. Who would've thought?"

Learning to Love the Lost Ones

"What do we do with all this stuff?" asked Jenny.

"Part of the healing comes from doing just what we've been doing," I replied. "Keeping up the facade takes a lot of energy. I think we all believe that we're the only one who's weird or screwed up. But when we share the parts of ourselves that we think are unacceptable and are, in fact, still accepted and loved by our friends, then something starts to soften. It's often easier for other people to be compassionate to us than it is for us to be compassionate to ourselves. As Pogo said, 'We've met the enemy and she is us.' Creating a more healthy and productive relationship with the shadow aspects of our psyche comes about primarily through changing our attitude. I think there's a clue in the Zulu story when the young woman is confronted by the horrible old woman's demand to lick her sores.

This strange act is a crucial moment in the story. The success or failure of this initiatory test depends on the young woman's willingness to intimately touch parts of the old woman that are repulsive. Through this process comes the strength and the wherewithal to meet and defend oneself from the monsters. Like a mother cat or dog, she uses her saliva for healing and cleansing. Saliva is also essential for digestion, and perhaps the sores on the old woman are like undigested parts of our being.

This story tells us that extraordinary gifts can come from our willingness to compassionately confront the parts of ourselves that we consider to be ugly and distasteful. From this single act, comes our liberation from the fate of being destroyed by the monster. Inanna, who Ereshkigal kills with her wrathful and evil gaze, is eventually rescued from the underworld through the efforts of two creatures. These creatures, created from the dirt underneath the God Enki's fingernails, come and sympathetically moan and groan with Ereshkigal who is in great pain and distress. Their compassion is such a relief to Ereshkigal that she rewards them by raising Inanna from the dead, who has been transformed through undergoing a ritual death and rebirth.

In both these stories, redemption comes through overcoming our inhibition to face the intolerable, as well as activating the compassionate heart. When we can love our ugliest parts, we are redeemed. We must then learn to love them unconditionally. If we cannot do this, the rejected parts begin to rage from their distant exile, creating a mess in the psyche.

One of the legacies left to me through my mother's death when I was still a child was a profound terror of being abandoned. When I became an adult I experienced severe, often irrational, anxiety about being left by the people I loved. I felt tremendous judgment toward this frightened and insecure aspect of my character and was ashamed that an otherwise strong and capable woman could be reduced to a quaking, terrified bundle of tears over seemingly nothing.

This vulnerable abandoned girl within plagued me for many years, until a close friend who knew about my internal battle confronted me about my attitude toward "the wounded one." He pointed out that my harsh judgment only aggravated the problem, and he suggested that I should learn compassion toward the small part of myself.

As I began to adopt a tenderer stance toward the frightened inner girl, she began to mellow out. She is always with me, but she does not rule the roost in the way she once did. From this I learned a valuable lesson about how to more effectively tend the shadowy parts of my feminine soul that do not always meet with my conscious approval.

I suggested to the Fierce Beauties that we start conversations with our inner crazy or wounded girls. Using the technique of active imagination, we can picture what she looks like and where she lives. Exploring this connection, we can discover what this part of us needs and respect the veracity of that information.

There is a sane logic behind much of what often seems to us like inappropriate or unacceptable behavior. In many ways, the crazy woman is like the canary in the mine that responds quickly to poisoned air. She lets us know when something is out of whack in our life. She will continue to irritate and generally confound the order of our daily lives unless we pay attention.

The crazy woman has a gift for us. She is a hole in us that is screaming to be filled. She is a river of tears waiting to be wailed. She is, above all else, in touch with the bedrock of the soul. Where we may have lost the thread of the truth of our being, the crazy woman does not forget. Her symptoms and expressions point the way toward true health.

The Zulu story teaches us that to become a woman, the adolescent girl must embrace the old woman with sores, who is really an aspect of herself. If she cannot, her feminine power will never be strong enough to withstand the monsters, which could be anyone or anything in her life that seeks to derail her from her dream. The monster can also come from within us through some part of us that sabotages our self-confidence and saps our vitality.

☀ Fierce Beauty Tip

Is there an aspect of your psyche that you dislike, are ashamed of, or embarrassed by? Using active imagination, visualize this part of you as a separate person. Notice what this person is wearing and doing. Enter into a dialogue with her, asking her what she needs. Notice your attitude toward her. Do you feel sympathetic or hostile, tender or harsh? Open your heart to this one who is in need of your compassion.

Mother Madness

One of the most frequent antagonists in the dramatic unfolding of a woman's original wound is her mother. Women's relationships with their mothers have a powerful influence on the way they form their identities. Our mothers are the templates on which we base our notions of what it means to be feminine. Some of this process happens consciously, through parental guidance and advice. More powerful, however, is the unconscious education transmitted through nonverbal body language, emotional currents, and, perhaps, even psychic channels.

Children absorb a great deal of who their parents are, for good or for bad. We assimilate the way our mothers feel about themselves as women. We inherit their angers, their frustrations, their grief and their insanity, as well as their yearnings and dreams. Linda Leonard writes that, "It is especially important to understand the sides of our mothers that we ignored, disliked, rejected, or feared, for this is often the first face of the feminine—and so the first face of the dark, mad side of the feminine—that we experience."

Like myself, many of my students and clients over the years have had some form of dysfunctional relationship with mothers who were alcoholics, mentally unstable, verbally and/or physically abusive, disempowered, abuse victims themselves, neglectful or simply uninvolved. We are the daughters of women who, in many cases, lost their way and walked unguided and alone amongst the ruins of social and familial arrangements that were no longer viable. We internalized the distortions of their unexpressed soul dreaming. Or, we rebelled against them and all things feminine in an effort to define ourselves distinctly without the encumbrance of being in their thrall.

Natalie Angier writes in her book *Woman* about how pervasive and unrelenting women's anger is toward their mothers. She suggests that one reason that daughters are so unforgiving is that, "The loss of the larger kinship matrix focuses the fury of our helplessness entirely on our mothers. We expect help from an older woman and our mother is the only older woman that we know." In a particularly cynical perspective, the authors of *Mother Daughter Revolution: From Betrayal to Power*, believe that mothers betray their daughters by being "conduits, and thus perpetuators of the dominant [patriarchal] culture."

Certainly, there are many reasons that women feel disappointed in their mothers. The most significant betrayal between mothers and daughters, however, is when mothers do not love and care for themselves adequately, and their daughters inescapably witness or bear the brunt of the consequences. A mother's suffering, regardless of whether it is expressed internally or externally, is intolerable for her young daughter to experience.

There comes a critical developmental juncture when a young girl desperately needs her mother to be whole, so that she can learn that wholeness herself. The fractured places in her mother are like fractured places in the earth itself. They are frightening, not only to her security in the present, but also because she intuitively knows that they threaten the formation of her future self. In a broken mirror, she sees only a distortion of her true self. When a young woman does battle with her mother, she is often fighting for her emotional survival.

I've had the dubious privilege of being both the blamer and the blamed. When I was 10 and 11 years old, I hated my mother for her weakness, her alcoholic bumbling and her pitiful postdrunk attempts to ameliorate the damage. Later in my life, my older daughter Tashina, at the age of 15, unmercifully and articulately accused me of transmitting my pain to her. With a very perceptive and unforgiving eye, we see our mothers in all their rawness, and we don't like some of what we see.

I've gone through various stages in relationship to my mother, which, although she is long gone, continues to change and grow with time and experience. For many years, after her death, I was numb. I remembered little about her, other than the bitter anger between us. As I began to delve into my psyche in my 20s, memories resurfaced. I became aware that at a core level, I blamed myself for her death—that my anger somehow killed her. This powerful belief affected me for many years. I thought something was terribly wrong with me, and I attempted to suppress any anger I might have toward the people around me, lest I cause them to die or leave as well.

I also discovered that a large portion of the feeling that I didn't want to be alive during this time of my life did not actually belong to me but, instead, to her. I had swallowed her grief and self-annihilation, like a white crane swallowing a fish whole. I remember being in a group therapy session where I imagined myself vigorously cleaning off dark cobwebs that enshrouded me, liberating my being from the legacy of her pain.

My anger at her for choosing to abandon her children persisted for many years. It lessened for a time after I became a mother myself and realized the difficult responsibility that she, as a mother of four children, had struggled with. But as I learned to mother my own children and tend my own soul at the same time, my anger returned. I could not, and perhaps would never understand what moved her to collapse so completely and abandon her four small daughters to the fates.

Finding Forgiveness

These days, I try to forgive my mother. It's not easy, but I've realized that the burning torch of my anger accomplished its mission. It motivated me out of nearly losing myself in a dark shadowy chasm of loss and self-hatred. It moved me into therapy, bodywork, and the loving nourishment of a circle of women. It catalyzed me to find spiritual sustenance.

I know now that forgiving and accepting my mother, with all her wounds, is an essential stage of tending my feminine soul. When we forgive our mothers, we have come full circle from rejecting the feminine, to accepting all its parts, both dark and light. Loving the broken mother is loving Ereshkigal in the underworld, and licking the old hag's sores. It's the same deal. Forgiveness cannot come falsely, however. Our anger is important. It has tremendous energy. We need that energy to transform. But to everything there is a season, and when the season of anger has passed, it is time to forgive. With forgiveness, comes integration. We become large enough to contain all aspects of the feminine soul.

Forgiving our mothers is not only an essential step for our personal healing, but also for the collective healing of the deep generational divisions in female culture. This process was brilliantly demonstrated in the movie, *One True Thing*, a story about the conflict-filled relationship between a traditional mother (Meryl Streep) and her professional daughter (Rene Zellweiger). The daughter comes home for a holiday visit only to discover that her mother is terminally ill. She ends up reluctantly staying to care for her mother and tend the household.

In the process, she learns something about the challenges and the value of her mother's world—a world she has disdainfully dismissed as being mundane and insignificant. She comes to respect her mother's compassionate service to the people around her, and her capacity to hold together the complex world of her family. From her mother, she also learns what it means to wholly love and commit to a man, in sickness and health, good times and bad. These qualities are very different from her fast-moving, competitive world of narcissistic pursuits and short-term liaisons.

The circumscribed roles of mothers and daughters can prevent us from seeing our mothers beyond their immediate relationship to us. But there are often complex dimensions to our mothers that we know little about. Dr. Paula Caplan, in *Don't Blame Mother*, suggests finding ways to humanize our mothers, "Thinking about mother as a person begins with the understanding that she did not magically appear in her full-blown, adult state, unrelated to her own childhood, the family who raised her, the wider environment in which she grew up, and the history of both her family and her culture."

Mother Gifts

It is essential to our well-being as women to identify not only the mother wound, but also the mother gift. Many of us have spent many long hours mucking around in the wound but little time exploring the good or helpful qualities that come to us through our mothers. I reminded the group that at the end of the Zulu story, the young woman is instructed to throw a stone into the river when she returns from being under the water, and asked them what that meant to them. As we pondered the meaning of this action, Elinor suggested, "I think the stone is a gift for the old woman in the bottom of the river. The young woman's been given a valuable life-changing lesson. She needs to honor the sources of her transformation."

"Maybe when we turn back toward our mothers and see them with different, more appreciative, eyes, we're throwing the stone in the pool," offered Alex. "We're acknowledging that they gave us a gift."

"What gift did you get from your mom, Liz?" asked Allison. She pulled the warm shawl that Sophie had lent her close around her neck and shoulders. Tendrils of coastal fog were eerily drifting in over the ridge top. "From everything that you've said, the whole scene sounded pretty much of a bummer."

"Well, that's true. But when I think about it, the best of who

I am came from her. She was a wild and passionate woman. She loved to sail and be near the ocean. She loved to dance. I remember her doing the limbo at parties—that Caribbean dance where they hold up a broom and people dance under it. As the dance goes on, the broom is lowered until it starts to get really hard to dance under it. She was also a very free-spirited woman, who loved to wear unusual clothes and be very theatrical. She was into literature and the arts. She and my father took me to see the ballet *Swan Lake* for my seventh birthday. I think she and I were cut from the same cloth. But there were a lot more options for expression available to me when I grew up than there were for her."

"That's similar to me and mi madre," Lena observed. "We've had a tough time over the years. But what I do and what she does are not that different. We both love to cook and look after other people, we've just done it in different ways. I've been very critical of her for taking so much crap from my dad and not doing anything for herself. But she kept our family together. When I think about it, I've relied on knowing that she's always there for me, making tortillas in her small kitchen, going to church and praying for my soul. Her heart is so big. It's the ground underneath me."

"I was closer to my Dad." Sylvia sat up and warmed her hands over the fire as she spoke. "My mother always wanted me to be a typical little girl with pretty dresses and patent leather shoes. I was more of a tomboy. I wanted to play out-doors out in the woods all the time. She would freak out when I came home with my dress covered with mud. My dad would let me come out and hang out in his workshop with him. He liked to repair antiques. I loved the smells of sawdust and paint varnish and the quiet way he had about him.

"I've realized lately, especially since joining this group, that I let my mother down. I've never really been a daughter to her and when I visit her I can see the hunger in her eyes. We had an interesting conversation the other day, though. She told me that she when she was younger, before she married my dad, she had aspired to be a newspaper reporter. She had worked as a journalist on her high school paper. I was amazed to hear this whole other side of my mom. She pays a lot of attention to current affairs. She reads two newspapers everyday. We've started having these great political discussions."

"My mom was a typical Jewish mother," said Sophie. "She used to drive me nuts. She was so bossy and overinvolved with my life. She was a very controlling woman. After she died, though, I realized how much I missed her. She really loved me. She was a strong woman, who knew her own mind and never hesitated to express her opinions. She intimidated me when I grew up. But she was a survivor who was determined that her family do well in America. I think of her indomitable will, sometimes, when I feel daunted by life."

☀ Fierce Beauty Tip

What gifts did your mother give you that you may not have recognized or acknowledged? Write a letter to her thanking her for all the gifts you have received along the way.

As we chatted about our complex relationships with our mothers, I thought wistfully that our mothers could have benefited enormously from a group like the Fierce Beauty Club. We were learning to give each other the strength and courage to descend into the dark and difficult realms of our inner and outer lives, find the jewels that resided in these depths, and then return with renewed strength and hope.

The last word of advice that the old woman in the river gives to the young girl is to not look back as she leaves the pool and returns to the village. This wisdom reminds us to make the descent, meet the challenge and then return enriched to our lives. The underworld has a powerful attraction and much to offer, but it is not a place to live. It is seductive for women, in particular, to get lost in the underworld, and they find it difficult to return. For those of us who wander too long in the muddy world of deep feeling, the myth warns us to complete our tasks and then move on.

In the story of Inanna's descent, she instructs a trusted friend, Ninshubur, in various ways to get her back if she does not return. When she fails to emerge from the underworld, Ninshubur perseveres until she gets the necessary help from the gods to resurrect Inanna. Similarly, when we explore the underworld, we should have the help and guidance of a trusted friend, therapist or women's circle to ensure that we do not lose our way. We can be Ninshuburs for one another by holding the container so that each person can do the work they need to do to meet and embrace their lost parts.

Ninshubur represents the ancient voice of the wisdom of Motherline that speaks to us through the voices of our close women friends. With an infallible sense of direction, in women's groups and in deep friendships, our friends help us to remember the way. They hold out the light that illuminates the path toward home. Through them, we are not lost. We are not abandoned. We are never really alone.

. . .

STEP 4: Reclaim the lost and forgotten parts of your psyche.

CHAPTER 5

Connecting with Our Fierce Beauty

To take much pleasure in a world filled with many kinds of beauty is a joy in life to which all women are entitled.

—Clarissa Pinkola Estés

THE SUN was just setting as the women arrived at Sophie's garage studio for our next meeting. Reluctant to go inside, we sat on the grass and watched the hills gradually change color from orange to pink to a deep mauve. As the twilight deepened, and the crickets began to sing, the barest sliver of a moon rose over the hill.

"It's so beautiful," said Jenny wistfully as she gazed out over the valley. "Quite a contrast to how I've been feeling lately."

Since Jenny's husband, Sam, had become involved with another woman, their marriage was barely surviving the stress. Despite couple's counseling and regularly attending the Fierce Beauty groups, her self-esteem was obviously still dragging on the ground like a bird with a broken wing.

"I wish we lived in a different kind of world," she continued angrily. "A world where you felt special and worthwhile, regardless of how old you are, or what you look like. It just doesn't seem fair. I feel like, because I no longer look a certain way, I don't have a ticket to get into the party anymore. I'm outside looking in the window at the 'beautiful girls' that have all the goodies."

Sophie affectionately wrapped her arm around Jenny and gave her a hug, saying, "I think we can all relate to that."

Over the months of meeting together, our friendships had strengthened and deepened. As we delved into our collective experience as women, we were learning the true value of creating female community together. Unraveling the tangled skein of our feminine identities, however, inevitably led us into many painful issues about our body images. As Jenny had expressed, most of us felt a great deal of pain and frustration about this issue. The next step in our journey together was to begin healing the shame and feelings of inadequacy that we felt about our bodies.

Chasing Impossible Dreams

The standard of beauty that our culture expects women to attain is increasingly impossible to achieve. Because of the enormous power of the media, we are bombarded by images of thin, young, glamorous women. Knowing that these images of women are often contrived through artificial techniques, such as airbrushing and lighting, does little to reduce the anxiety that they produce in most women.

- 75% of women between the ages of 18 and 35 *believe* that they are overweight, while only 25% are actually medically overweight.

- Twenty years ago, models weighed 8% less than the average woman, today they weigh 23% less.

- Only 3% of the female population even has the appropriate bone structure to attempt to conform to this Barbie doll standard.

Surgical interventions to remake women into the idealized culturally accepted form of beauty are one of the fastest growing medical specialties in this country. In the 1997 Miss America pageant, 41 out of 51 contestants had undergone breast augmentation. Nose jobs, liposuctions, collagen injections, chin and cheekbone recontouring, and even the removal of ribs are now common procedures for pageant contestants. It seems that, as a culture, we are moving farther and farther away from an appreciation of natural beauty and closer to an alien form of beauty that is manipulated and contrived through artificial means.

Our culture's bias toward masculinity has also influenced our idea of the "perfect" female form. Over the past 30 years, women's desired body types have steadily become thinner, harder and more muscular. Since 1991, steroid use to increase muscle tone and bulk among young women has risen 100 percent. Like Demi Moore in the movie *G.I. Jane* and Linda Hamilton in *Terminator 2*, our bodies are increasingly supposed to look more male. The zaftig, sensual body types of movie stars of the 1940s and 1950s, such as Marilyn Monroe, who wore a size 16, are a thing of the past. Our culture is losing love and respect for its naturally round, soft female bodies.

As women grow older, our access to beauty power lessens. Most women over the age of 50 feel invisible. In fact, most of us who are approaching our middle years feel that it is unacceptable to age. We dye our hair and work out to counteract the natural softening and rounding that comes with age. I can foresee the time when surgical aids to maintain youth will be the norm for women rather than the exception.

As we discussed this issue in the group that night, Lena said, "I feel so hopeless about this." She made herself comfortable in one of the overstuffed chairs in the studio. "It's hard to know where to begin to make any real changes. Our society is so messed up. Sometimes I just want to go live on a desert island with no mirrors, men or movies with their Hollywood babes in my face all the time."

"Look at us! We're a reasonably well-educated group of women. We've read all the books. All they do is talk about the problem without offering any solutions. We all seem to *know* what the problem is, but we don't have a clue how to change it."

How do we heal the beauty wound, whose tentacles wrap around our collective psyche, smothering our joy and confidence? Many of us, like Lena, feel helpless in our attempts to overcome the adverse effects on our self-esteem and our relationships. We tend to get together and rant impotently about men's sexual obsessions and the exploitative state of the media. There are, however, concrete steps that women can take to liberate themselves from this death-like grip, through addressing the dysfunctional effects of the beauty wound on the multiple levels of body, mind, spirit and emotion.

Beyond the Boogeyman

A crucial first step for the Fierce Beauty Club was to stop wasting our time blaming men or other abstract forces in society that were beyond our control. Many of us believe that men are the ones holding us to this unreasonable standard of beauty. Through my gender reconciliation work, however, I've discovered that many men also feel victimized by the Beauty Game. They report feeling confused and manipulated by the unending barrage of media images of women that are created just to hook their sexual imagination.

Society indoctrinates men at an early age that true success as a man comes from scoring the Playboy bunny model who may be advertising the Lexus that he wants. The movies and television are filled with scenarios in which men repeatedly make bad and sometimes dangerous decisions because they have fallen under the spell of a sexually attractive woman. Like Pavlov's dog, they are programmed to respond to certain stimuli. It is not uncommon for older men, like Jenny's husband, to throw away their lives to pursue some cute young thing instead of staying involved with a real woman who could actually be a good partner and lover.

On the other hand, many men are less concerned with beauty than women think. According to one survey of male attitudes, men are not as fixated on large breasts as women think. Interviewing both men and women about what each thinks the ideal breast size is for women, women believe that men prefer a much larger size than, in fact, they actually do. The majority of men in our workshops say that humor, playfulness and self-confidence are more important to them than appearance. In long-term relationships, they say a woman's beauty actually plays a small role. Most men, however, will admit that what primarily attracts their *initial* interest is, in fact, a woman's looks.

We are undoubtedly influenced by thousands of years of social and biological behavior patterns governing relations between women and men. Evolutionary psychologists increasingly believe that ancient genetic mandates still influence men to select certain types of women for the successful propagation of the species. This may be at the root of some of the more deeply habitual male tendencies to stare at or make sexual advances toward younger women with well-defined hips and breasts. But regardless of the root cause of the beauty wound, blaming men exclusively is a misunderstanding of the depth and complexity of the problem and its adverse effects on both sexes.

As we continued arguing about men and beauty, Lena produced a plate of cookies and a bowl of ripe red strawberries for us to munch on. "I think we're going to need some serious sustenance to get through this," she joked.

"When I think about it, men checking out a woman's body is not that different from a woman checking out how much money a guy makes before she'll even date him," countered Allison, passing the plate of cookies to Sylvia. "Hey, how many of us were looking for that guy with the upscale car and the fat bank roll in his pocket?"

"But we do give our power away to men when it comes to this issue. I know I have," I asserted. "I spent a lot of years waiting for some man to make me feel beautiful enough. I thought men had some kind of a magic wand that would turn me from a frog into a princess."

"Not that you look much like a frog, Liz," Lena said, as she playfully poked me with her elbow.

"I know what she's saying though. What a colossal waste of time!" exclaimed Sylvia. She jumped up and agitatedly paced around the room. "Are we going to spend a lifetime pursuing a magic feeling that only comes from having our beauty adored by some guy? The longer I wait and the more expectations I have, the angrier I get."

Clearly men can't solve this problem for us. An ongoing challenge for the Fierce Beauties was to find ways to reject victimhood and reclaim our power as women. We'd worked hard on this in our previous groups. Now it was time to heal the beauty wound for ourselves. In the safety of our group, in the company of girlfriends, we could take the necessary steps to redefine beauty and claim our inherent right to feel beautiful. We could create a new model of beauty that was accessible to all women.

As women in search of fierce beauty, we need the help of other women to see and feel our own depth and true beauty. We need each other's help to overcome the negativity most of us feel about our bodies. The Fierce Beauty Club showed us that we can be mirrors for one another—mirrors that reflect heart, tenderness, strength, sensuality and fierce wild beauty, instead of the cold, hard edges of media images of "perfect" women with no connection to their souls.

☀Fierce Beauty Tip

Discover what men actually think about the beauty standard by interviewing several men that you come in contact with. Find out what their considerations are when they pick a romantic partner. Compare their feedback with the assumptions you may have made, and keep notes in your Fierce Beauty journal.

Beauty = Power

In my private consulting work, I've noticed that it is rare to come across a woman, even one who is beautiful by society's standards, who feels that she is attractive enough. The beauty wound is one of the largest holes in the fabric of female identity. Confidence and self-esteem leak out of this breach in the feminine soul at an appalling rate. Despite feminist efforts to educate us that a woman's worth is more than the sum of her body parts, most women still secretly believe that beauty is the primary source of their power.

I have observed that some women who are obsessed with external beauty are also fascinated with power. They seek to hone their beauty power as a means of controlling or dominating their world. And while there is nothing wrong with women's will to power, we have never openly acknowledged the extent of this inner drive to each other or the world. Owning up to it is an important part of understanding and transforming our relationship to external beauty when it becomes unhealthy.

The "Beauty = Power" formula is deeply entrenched in our psyches. It evokes a primal fear that if a woman lacks sufficient beauty, she will not attract a man who will provide her with food, shelter and emotional sustenance. Although women have made great progress in becoming more financially independent, the belief that "I must be beautiful" to really succeed still creates an underlying anxiety for many of us. This fear actually may increase as our interest in gaining economic power grows.

It is true that in the past beauty power was one of the only avenues available for women to achieve power. This type of power is, however, elusive and transitory by nature, available only to a minority of women for a limited period of life. It also binds women to an unhealthy bargain with men in which their lives are lived indirectly, and often unsuccessfully, through the destiny of their male partner. Achieving power through external beauty is often an unholy pursuit of a false god, to the detriment of our bodies and our souls.

Reclaiming Soul Beauty and Personal Magic

The next task in women's recovery is to redefine the true nature of beauty. Psychologist James Hillman says, "That revelation of soul's essence...is called in mortal language, beauty." He goes on to say that beauty is the "way that the Gods touch our senses, reach the heart and attract us into life...and that if beauty is inherent and essential to soul, then beauty appears wherever soul appears." Thomas Moore in *The Soul of Sex* describes beauty as a kind of radiance or luminosity. By this definition, when women align with their souls, they *become* beautiful and more powerful.

Jungian writer Christine Downing suggests that this soul beauty is personified by the Greek goddess Aphrodite, whose "beauty is connected to your goldenness, your warmth, your availability. That energy is *charis*, grace . . . that energy is charisma, personal magic." This quality of personal magic emanates from a connection with the feminine soul. When this charismatic soul beauty is present in a woman, she attracts others through evoking joy and enthusiasm for life. If true beauty is the same as personal magic, then instead of putting enormous amounts of time and money into refining our appearance, we could commit all that time and resources to the tending of our souls. We might then achieve a more lasting and unique beauty that is the result of doing what we love, living out our dreams and following our deepest passions for life.

"So Liz, let me get this right," said Allison skeptically. She warmed her hands over the crackling fire as the evening cooled off. "You're saying that all we have to do is be in tune with ourselves and we'll be beautiful?"

"I think what she's saying is that we have to find a way to be happy, because, when we do what we love, that makes us more beautiful," offered Sophie.

Sophie went on, "My old grandma had that kind of soul beauty. When I was a kid, I used to visit her in Pennsylvania.

She would always take me out to work with her in her vegetable garden. I remember thinking how beautiful she was sitting in the dirt, with her bare feet, and strong hands weeding and digging. She loved that garden with all her heart. It's where her soul came alive."

"I've seen you look like that when you paint, Sophie," I said. "You're covered with paint and happy as a kid playing with mud pies. Your red hair seems to crackle with electricity and your cheeks get all rosy. You practically vibrate with energy."

"Maybe that's why Michael always seems more interested in making in love after I've been out here painting," she answered slyly, her eyes sparkling with private thoughts.

"I think this new definition of beauty is exciting. It actually makes me feel hopeful," Sylvia added. "I like the idea of personal magic. It's accessible. It makes the pursuit of beauty more of a spiritual or a creative quest than a physical one."

Instead of rigid, narrow-minded and limiting ideas of visual beauty that injure our bodies and souls, soul beauty arises from physical and psychological health as well as spiritual alignment. Soul beauty calls us to listen to the voices within that can move us into a more meaningful and fulfilling existence. The direction of the Fierce Beauties' quest was now to go inward to discover what truly brought us joy and what unique feminine magic we contributed to our world.

I suggested we do an exercise in which each woman took a turn telling us about what she loved doing most in her life. We spent the rest of the evening sharing what really turned us on and made us feel truly alive. For some of us it was doing simple things like working in our garden or cooking. For Sophie, it was, of course, her painting. Alex told us how much she loved building her small business, that the challenge of solving multiple problems made her feel the thrill of the chase. As each woman spoke about her passions, I noticed that she became animated and energized. Her cheeks filled with color and her eyes glimmered. Jenny's chronically hunched shoulders lifted. Lena's ample chest shook with laughter. Their external appearance lit up with internal soul beauty as they expressed their creative enthusiasm.

☀Fierce Beauty Tip

Think of all the things you do that you love. Imagine yourself doing one of these activities. Notice the way you feel. Experience the energy that streams through your being as you engage in life with full enthusiasm. This is your magic, your luminosity, and your soul beauty. Do this visualization whenever you feel out of touch with your soul beauty.

Revealing the Wound

The next and more difficult step in the process of recovering true beauty is to uncover the depth of the pain that so many of us feel about our bodies. It is deeply healing for women to honestly admit to other women the extent of their body hatred. It works in the same mysterious way as does confession in the Catholic Church, self-revelation in AA recovery groups, and for many, talking to a psychotherapist.

For many women, the roots of their negative self-image reach far back into the past. We often learn from our own mothers—who were in turn taught by their mothers—that a woman's job is to refine her beauty as a means of attracting a man to take care of her. Some of us also had demoralizing experiences with our fathers, other children, siblings or boyfriends. Most of us, however, have a particular memory of an event that started us down the path of disliking our bodies. Discovering that core event helps begin unwinding the subsequent damage.

One of the most common scenarios that I hear reported by clients and students is the degree to which our mothers significantly influenced the way in which we formed our self-image.

When our mothers lose their self-esteem and become lost in their own body hate, we daughters catch it like an infectious disease. Sometimes this happens indirectly through witnessing our mother's personal struggle with self-image. In other cases, mothers become tyrannical forces in their daughters' lives, projecting their own insecurities onto their daughters' vulnerable young psyches.

One of my earliest memories is of watching my mother, who had given birth to four children—three by cesarean section—struggle to stuff her scarred and stretched-out belly into a girdle. That memory has shadowed me my entire life. Her own shame about her body, marked with the battle scars of motherhood, taught me that there was something wrong with my own belly, because it also was not flat and hard.

Allison, the youngest member of our group, told us the story of her destructive relationship with her mother. She confessed to us that for years she had been bulimic—controlling her weight by vomiting after she ate. The revelation that this young, attractive woman with a "perfect" body was paying such a terrible price to maintain her looks stunned the group. She told us, "My mother was a gorgeous woman. When I was growing up, she was constantly on a diet. Later on she became a feminist and renounced all this beauty stuff, but at that time she was completely obsessed with her looks. When I was about 10 years old, I started to get a little plump. Mom forced me to go on her diet. My life with her became a constant battle of wills.

"I would sneak out and buy candy, bring it back into my room, and then pig out. She would find wrappers or crumbs and then punish me by grounding me for weeks at a time. My life became obsessed with food. When I was about 14, I realized I could binge and then purge. At first it was out of defiance of my mother. But then it became something I couldn't stop."

Women who fall short of society's beauty standards are not the only ones who struggle with unrealistic expectations of beauty. In my work with clients, I've discovered, to my surprise, that many young women, *especially* very "attractive" women, obsessively drive themselves to be thinner and more muscular. A survey done at our local university indicated that an astonishing 23 percent of their female students suffer with some type of eating disorder, including anorexia, bulimia, compulsive exercising and excessive dieting. In *Fasting Girls*, Joan Jacobs Brumberg estimates that at certain college campuses one in five women is anorexic or bulimic.

I thought back to a memory of Leah, a dark-eyed woman in her middle 30s, who was a participant at a workshop that I taught focusing on enhancing self-esteem and self-image. It was held at a beautiful retreat center in the mountains above Santa Barbara. She wore a halter-top revealing a tiny waist, small breasts and a slim body. In a quiet voice with tears running down her cheeks, Leah told me about her experiences growing up.

"My father left my mother when I was about eight years old. We moved to Los Angeles and even though we were poor, we always had perfect clothes. There was hardly any food in the house, but we had the finest designer outfits. I learned early on from my mother that I better look good if I wanted to make it in this world. I became obsessed with losing weight. When I was 14 I only weighed 85 pounds.

"I allow myself to eat now. But I still hate certain parts of my body that aren't as thin as I would like, especially my thighs. I never wear shorts and I am very careful not to let my boyfriend see them, if I can help it, even when we make love. It's hard to believe that there is anything more to me than what I look like." She confessed, "I still spend some days totally hating myself, because I feel fat. I get so obsessed with my outside appearance that I can't even feel myself inside. I don't know who I am, other than what I look like."

When we open up like this with other women, we stop

pretending that we are okay, because in truth, we aren't. Letting go into our feelings, we surrender the persona—the false self we attempted to create. Releasing the emotions attached to painful experiences that we may have carried with us for years creates the opening for new, more constructive, patterns to form. This is not impotent wailing at our plight but a healthy grieving process necessary to moving forward into the future.

☀Fierce Beauty Tip

Get together with a trusted woman friend and take turns telling each other all the negative beliefs you have about your body. Tuning into the deep feelings you may have, let it all out. Release the frustrations, the wounds, the anger, the grief and the burden you've carried of trying to live up to an impossible beauty standard.

Coming Home to Ourselves

The unseen price of our cultural obsession with external beauty is that many women, like Leah, lose touch with their interiority—a sense of inner reality that is connected with their hearts, their intelligence and, ultimately, with their souls. Rita Freedman, in her book *Beauty Bound,* says that many women suffer a kind of "psychic annihilation." When we focus entirely on what we look like and how we are seen, some essential part of our inner being becomes increasingly invisible and often disappears altogether. Like Narcissus in the Greek myth, who wasted away while contemplating his face in a pool of water, women's souls waste away as they critique themselves mercilessly in front of a mirror.

Recovering from the beauty wound demands that women redirect their awareness from their outside appearance to their inside experience. This shift in focus is not easy. After all, we're attempting to break a chain of behavior that's been going on a long time. It takes will power and regular supportive contact with other women who can help each other remember to, as poet Cassandra Light says, "peel yourself off the mirror." Within us lies a fertile garden that can provide us with a much more nourishing, rewarding and sustainable source of information about our personal value. I recommend to women that they swear off mirrors for a while (that includes store windows and other reflective surfaces) in order to start feeling their insides.

☀Fierce Beauty Tip

Just for a lark, see how long you can go without looking in a mirror. What other reference points do you have to measure your beauty? Pay particular attention to body sensations, emotional states and energy levels.

There are a variety of exercises that women can do together to help each other reconnect with an internal experience of soul beauty. For example, removing each other's makeup allows our true self to be seen and mirrored in a new, more compassionate way. During our next weekly meeting of the Fierce Beauty Society, we decided to look at one another's faces without our makeup masks. We revealed our true faces to each other.

"This is so hard to do," exclaimed Alex. "I feel naked. I'm so used to putting on my face before I even see my family in the morning."

"No kidding," said Sylvia. "It's very uncomfortable for me to let you all see what I really look like. I guess I am ashamed of my face. I can hardly bear to do this."

Allowing ourselves to be truly seen is very provocative for some women and a deeply intimate experience. Many women won't ever allow another human being to see their faces without makeup. We hide our true vulnerable faces and bodies behind makeup, jewelry and clothing. But although we are afraid to be seen, we are paradoxically desperate to be seen.

✳Fierce Beauty Tip

Get together with a close woman friend and take turns gently and lovingly removing each other's makeup. Spend a few minutes looking at each other without your usual masks. Notice how it feels to be truly seen by another person. Share your feelings and reactions.

In her book, *The Power of Beauty,* Nancy Friday talks about the power of the "Gaze," which we ideally receive as infants from our mothers and fathers. Receiving the Gaze means being held with love in the eyes of another. It is the act of being cherished. And it is essential for babies to develop and mature in a healthy way. The eyes are a primary vehicle for the parent to convey value and worth to the child. Many of us, however, did not adequately receive the Gaze from our parents. If our beauty was not reflected to us as small children, then as adults, we become terribly hungry for this confirmation from others.

If we miss the opportunity to be seen by parents, then, as we discussed before, many of us will search desperately for this Gaze from men. We may also spend a great deal of time in front of a mirror, attempting to give ourselves the Gaze. Self-gazing is usually ineffective, however, because most of us habitually see ourselves with critical eyes rather than with love.

The healing gaze of women in a safe and gentle setting has a potent effect. I've seen its power repeatedly in my groups. It allows a woman to have the opportunity to become a vulnerable young girl again. This young girl yearns to be recognized for all of who she is. Without this Gaze she may never become a whole woman, and will be forever caught in a netherworld of unformed, unrealized possibility.

"You know Alex, your face looks so much softer without your makeup," Elinor told her as she used tissues to clean away the last remaining makeup on Alex's face. In the soft light, she gently wiped off the jade green eye shadow that Alex was fond of. "You actually look younger. You have a freshness that I never noticed before."

"Even though doing this is hard, it feels kind of good," responded Alex.

Alex and Elinor switched and Alex began to tenderly wash Elinor's face. "I have so many lines," apologized Elinor. "I don't even like to look in the mirror any more. I can't accept the face that I see there. Inside, I feel younger than 71. But outside I feel like an ugly old hag."

"Oh Elinor," Alex argued, stroking her cheeks, "I hate it when you talk like that. You have a beautiful face. I hope I look like you when I'm your age. There's so much wisdom and depth in your face."

Not only has the beauty wound caused deep rifts between mothers and daughters, it has also historically torn apart many women's friendships. Because beauty feels scarce, fleeting and hard-won to most of us, competition between women, particularly older and younger women, in this arena is cutthroat. A more useful strategy, however, is for women to assist one another in creating opportunities to fill in the holes that developed through living in families and communities that inadequately provided safe passages for young girls to become women. We can be mothers for one another, conferring beauty and acceptance with the power of our eyes. In this way we can birth a new sense of ourselves and our worth that is based upon recognition of our unique soul beauty.

Fierce Beauty Tip

As you go through your day, notice when you judge other women's beauty critically. Practice *seeing* beauty in faces and bodies that you would ordinarily dismiss. Look for grace, radiance, wisdom, vitality and strength in the faces and bodies you meet.

Loving All Our Parts

The next step in healing the beauty wound is for women to explore their own negative attitudes toward their bodies. One way to begin this process is to identify a particular part of your body that you especially dislike. In the Fierce Beauty group, the women shared the memories they had connected with that body part, the shameful images, and the nasty critical remarks that they, or another person, may have made to themselves about this part of their body. For several of the women it was their stomachs. Sylvia hated her height and her big bones. Jenny hated the size of her breasts. She resorted to wearing big over-sized clothes much of her life to cover up her body. Sophie's "ugly part" was her face, particularly her nose and, more recently, the growing webbing of lines around her eyes and her mouth.

"I've always been self-conscious about my nose," she told us. "I was teased as a child. They used to call me Pinocchio at school." Her eyes filled as she remembered. "God, kids can be cruel. I had red hair and a big nose. I would have given anything for a nose job, but my parents couldn't afford it. And now I'm getting all these lines, its horrible. Whenever I see myself in the mirror, I go 'Yuck.'"

"You know what would feel good right now? Could all of you put your hands on my face and head? It would feel so good to have you touch me."

As the women gathered around her and gently touched her face, Sophie began to cry as she said, "I feel so much relief. It's as if your touch is taking away all the years I've spent hating my face."

Like the Gaze, the power of touch is another vehicle for women to heal the beauty wound in one another. As with our eyes, we convey love, acceptance and unconditional positive regard through our touch. Allowing the "ugly parts" of us to be touched by another with love has the effect of melting away long-held tensions and pockets of negativity. This nonsexual, healing expression of human connection can be done in the safety of a close group of women friends, as well as with husbands and lovers or even professional body workers.

Women are so often critical of their parts that they begin to lose connection with their entire bodies. A gentle touch helps us to come back into ourselves. We can then reintegrate the parts of ourselves that we have always wished would change or disappear.

"If you imagine your ugly part as being a child in your family, how are you treating this child?" I asked the women.

"Like Cinderella, the ugly stepsister," answered Allison.

"Or shunned and made to sit in a dark closet," said Sylvia.

"Mine is one of those children you read about in the paper that's discovered locked up in a back room, half-starved and unwashed for years," added Lena.

Our ugly parts are like members of our family that we find unacceptable. We are verbally if not physically abusive to these parts. We lock them up in closets, starve them, force food into them, bind them, cut on them and only allow them out of the house with masks on. What if we were compassionate, gentle, affirming and loving to these parts of ourselves instead of shaming and castigating?

Healing the beauty wound requires an attitude adjustment. We need to become loving parents to our body parts. One way to accomplish this is to become more aware of our "self-talk"—

the unconscious stream of inner dialogue that we say to ourselves as we go through our lives. For many women, this self-talk tends to be highly critical and a reflection of our deepest beliefs about ourselves. We say little nasty things to ourselves about our appearance, our body parts and other character traits that we don't like such as "You fat blimp," or "God, you look like an old hag today."

Recovering from the disease of body hate requires making a conscious and disciplined effort to transform our deprecating self-talk into a more loving affirmation of our worth. I suggested to the group that they develop some positive affirmations that they could substitute for their negative self-talk. Repeating affirmations about our beauty and worth is another way to learn to love and appreciate our bodies.

"It's hard to think of one, Liz," responded Lena. "I've been eating a steady diet of put-downs for so long."

"What about something like, 'I enjoy my body' or 'I love the shape of my body'?" offered Sophie.

"Or, 'my body feels good to me today' might be a good one," I added.

Fierce Beauty Tip

Notice which part or parts of your body you particularly dislike. Search your past memories of growing up in a female body and see if there is a particular formative event that created this wound in your body image. Practice appreciating this body part every time you find yourself being critical. Touch that part of your body lovingly. Try doing this each night for a week. See if your attitude begins to shift.

Discovering the Sensual Body

One of the greatest mistakes women make is the extent to which we dwell on *looking* beautiful, rather than *feeling* beautiful. It is as if we spend all our time decorating and improving a home that nobody lives in. Or repeatedly polishing a silver bowl that is never used to hold food. When we exist outside ourselves, constantly looking critically at our image, we lose the true source of beauty—a healthy relationship with our female sensual body—liking what it does, how it feels, the way it moves, the way it smells.

"When do you feel beautiful?" I asked the women. We were all relaxing on brightly colored cushions on the floor of the studio. The night was warm, and we left the door open to let the breeze to come in.

"I don't know what you mean, Liz," replied Jenny. "I don't know if I've ever *felt* beautiful."

"Well, what if we spent more time paying attention to being more sensual, instead of more beautiful? What kinds of experiences make you feel really good?" I asked again.

"I remember when I was in Hawaii a year ago," mused Lena. "I dressed up in a really soft fabric sarong. I spent some time in the ocean and lying in the sun. The pores of my skin felt like they were vibrating. There was a gentle breeze blowing around me that smelled like flowers. In that moment I felt absolutely beautiful. Who knows what I looked like, but I felt like a goddess. I actually got up and started dancing on the beach, swaying like the palm trees in the wind. No one in that moment could have told me I wasn't beautiful."

"That's nice for you," Jenny snorted sarcastically. "The only time I went to Hawaii, I spent most of my time feeling uncomfortable and self-conscious in my bathing suit on the beach, wishing I was some skinny, young thing. I was so uptight about my body that I couldn't even enjoy the wonderful place that I was in. I could have been running and playing in the waves instead of hiding under my beach blanket."

"Don't you think we're missing out on life when hating our bodies keeps us from having fun?" I suggested.

"I've been thinking about what went wrong in my marriage," Jenny confided. "After I had children, I lost interest in our sex life. Part of it was because I had these babies hanging on me all day and I had a hard time shifting gears at night. But I also gained weight when I was pregnant and I felt unattractive to my husband. When we did make love I spent most of the time making sure that Sam couldn't see my belly or my thighs."

"That doesn't sound like much fun," Alex remarked, as she added another pillow to the already large pile underneath her. "So, if you're not a Victoria's Secret model, you can't have a good sex life?"

"We got this all wrong, girlfriends," I said. "I worked with a woman who was overweight and miserable. She really wanted a guy but nothing ever seemed to last with the men she dated. During the time we worked together she got into ballroom dancing, which she totally loved. She told me that when she was dancing she felt beautiful. Men started asking her to dance and to go out, and now she has a lover that she's having a great time with. She didn't lose any weight, but her relationship to her body changed. She became more at ease in herself."

Sensuality is very attractive to men. I believe it is actually *more* consistently and enduringly attractive to men than external superficial beauty. *All women can be sensual beings if they want to.* It is a quality that we cultivate through paying attention to the body and what it likes. Sensuality comes from the Latin word meaning "to feel." We develop it through developing our sensory body awareness. Some of the many ways this can be achieved are through:

1. All kinds of dance and movement
2. Experiencing massage and other kinds of bodywork
3. Nonobsessive exercise such as walking, yoga and swimming.
4. Eating a delicious meal
5. Using a hot tub or bathing in bubble bath
6. Discovering clothing that evokes a sensual feeling, such as soft, draping fabrics
7. Going out into nature and receiving it with all your senses

We are all different and thus all have our own unique forms of sensual expression. The most important thing is to keep returning our focus and attention to creating opportunities to feel beautiful, rather than just looking beautiful. Sensuality is not limited by age. In fact, if a woman is at home in the temple of her body, discovering its delights as she lives, her sensuality will only grow as she gets older. On the island of Haiti, in a culture that deeply values music and dance, they believe that the best dancers are the old women, because they have lived so much life.

One warm summer day, the Fierce Beauties took a trip together to a hot spring located way back in the hills of Los Padres National Forest. After hiking up a trail for about a mile through fields of sweet-smelling lupine, we finally reached a lovely set of pools tucked into the hillside, surrounded by ferns and palm fronds. The creek that ran into the hot sulfur pools gently burbled. Since no one was around, we took off our clothes and surrendered to the warm water. When we got too warm we lay on the boulders around the pools and occasionally, with loud shrieks, bravely dipped in the freezing cold creek.

"Ah, this is divine," said Sylvia, her long body draped over an oblong rock that seemed to be perfectly made for her.

"In this moment I guess I could say that I feel beautiful, Liz," added Jenny, who resembled some kind of nature sprite with her head peeking out from between a bank of ferns.

Nature is one of the most powerful antidotes to the ill effects of the beauty wound. It takes us away from the incessant stream of images, from mirrors of all kinds and from the habitual patterns that reinforce our negative body image. In nature, we evoke the more wild, elemental part of ourselves—an ancient memory that is not bound by culture or family. The more time women spend in nature, the more connected they become to the sensate body—the body that knows that it is healthy and can move through the world with grace and ease.

Dancing the Light Fantastic

In nature, as well as the safe container of our circle, the Fierce Beauties affirmed their right to be erotic, to love and feel beautiful in their bodies. We tried various exercises back at home and in the group to rediscover our sensuality. One night, a few weeks later, we explored our own unique interpretations of what it meant to be "sexy" by dressing up in wild, colorful, erotic costumes and dancing together to rock and roll. Jenny surprised us all by showing up in a leopard skin spandex body suit and a black boa, with exotic black kohl eyeliner highlighting her large brown eyes. Alex wore a deep purple kimono with white cranes embroidered on it over a long white silk dress.

"Wow, look at you!"

"Turn around, let me see the back."

"Where did you get that boa?"

The women oohed and ahhed as we took turns strutting and preening around the room. They started putting gold and silver glitter on each other's faces. It delighted me to see each of them laughing and playing together, more at ease in their bodies than ever before. Many women dress up for men as a means of attracting their attention. Their sense of style develops through attuning themselves to what they think men will find desirable. On the other hand, many women get so disgusted with that pressure that they rebel by refusing to dress up at all. In reaction to the beauty game, they restrain and inhibit their sensual and erotic style.

In the safety of our group, the Fierce Beauties gave each other the permission to discover our own unique style that is not about being something for anyone other than ourselves. The women began to blossom and emerge from a long winter of shame and emotional starvation. I saw the plump women get up and dance in front of other women, displaying their ample bodies with pride and joy. I saw Elinor step out of the shrouds of invisibility and become a glorious, sensual, elder beauty. I saw a young woman who was rigidified into a plastic mannequin, get down and become a funky, warm, sexy bundle of life, enjoying the pleasure of being connected with her own sensual female body.

☀Fierce Beauty Tip

Explore your own unique style of displaying your sensuality. Play with different kinds of clothing and fabrics to discover what makes you feel the most deliciously and erotically sensual. Pay more attention to how you feel than how you look.

In recent years I've worked with these steps to heal my own beauty wound. We teach what we need to learn. I noticed as a teenager that certain women, by virtue of the way they looked, were able to command the attention and resources of the world around them. As a woman intrigued by power and desirous of men's appreciation, I knew that I wanted that mysterious commodity we call beauty. "Got to get me some of that," I repeated to myself like a mantra.

As a reasonably attractive woman by society's standards, I possessed enough of this precious substance to be successful with men. But as I got older and had two children, abdominal surgery and a busy life that precluded three hours a day working out at the gym, I felt the first whispers of fear begin to wrap cold fingers around my gut. Maybe I, like other women I knew, would also become undesirable, irrelevant and unseen. I worried that my husband might lose interest in me at some point. Perhaps not being beautiful *enough* would consign me to a life of loneliness.

Being stubborn and contentious by nature, however, I finally just refused to go down that road. I started searching for a different kind of beauty and power that would sustain me, and other women as well, throughout our lives. Now when that mosquito whine of the "I am not thin enough/pretty enough" voice starts buzzing in my ear, I know that I have to go back to the tools that will restore me to the right connection with my inner soul beauty and my sensual body. These steps are not a one-time healing panacea, however, they are more of an ongoing discipline.

It is easy for me, as well as most women that I know, to lose this connection. The beauty standard is extremely powerful, and aging is inexorable. The cultural momentum of the media and collective attitudes that surround us, frequently pull me out of an internal sense of balance. In order to remember where true beauty comes from, I have to resist that pressure and drop back into the deep, essential parts of myself. I have to remind myself that if I feel unbeautiful it is not because I have gained a few pounds or gray hairs. It is because I am out of sync with the timeless wisdom of my feminine soul and the organic rhythms of my sensual body.

From the experience of doing this work with the Fierce Beauty Club and other women, I know for a certainty that we can heal the wounds we feel about our beauty. We can release the pain of past self-hate and learn how to truly love all the parts of our bodies. Discovering our personal magic, we make space for our deepest dreams to come true. Through finding a new, more fulfilling relationship with our sensual body, we learn how to feel beautiful and enjoy the pleasures available to us through the senses. And with the strength, love and support of female community, women can sustain this new experience of beauty throughout the passages of their lives and pass it along to the daughters who follow.

. . .

STEP 5: Connect with your soul beauty and sensuality.

CHAPTER 6

Celebrating Our Sacred Sexuality

A woman becomes a Sex Goddess not by virtue
of a perfect body, a bag of exotic tricks, or a
Valentino-like lover, but by virtue of her ability
to abandon herself to the electrically sensual
qualities of everything around and within her.
—Olivia St. Claire

WE ARRIVED at Sylvia's house around dinnertime for our first overnight meeting. She lived in a small frame house that was one of a row of well-kept but modest houses with manicured gardens filled with bougainvillaea, and jasmine. She had suggested we carpool due to a shortage of parking. After fitting narrowly into a tight space that we had only found after making oblations to the parking gods, Sophie, Elinor, Lena and I schlepped various bundles into the house.

"What on earth did you bring?" I asked Lena, as we returned to Elinor's van for the second time. "You name it, I brought it," she replied. We carried sleeping bags, pillows, food, videos, CDs, and an assortment of skin care supplies up to the house. "I want to do facials and pedicures, watch chick flicks, listen to rock and roll and eat. We're gonna have a good time," she affirmed with enthusiasm.

At the end of our last meeting, Allison had suggested we get together and have a slumber party. "Just like when we were kids," she proposed. So here we were, preparing for what we hoped might become an annual event. It was a big deal for most of us to take this much time out of our busy schedules and away from our families. As we all gathered, there was a feeling of exhilaration and anticipation.

"I feel like I just barely escaped," Alex reported. "My youngest was complaining of a sore throat as I left, but Danny insisted that he could handle it, bless his heart. I feel a little guilty, but nothing I can't handle."

Sylvia's house was simply but elegantly decorated. The main part of the house was a large living space with the kitchen area and a dining table in one corner. Various artifacts and pictures that appeared to be from Africa were placed thoughtfully around.

"I didn't know you were so interested in African art," I commented to Sylvia as we put food in the refrigerator.

"Oh yes," she shared. "Ever since I was a child, I've been fascinated with Africa. One of these days I'm going to get myself there."

After getting a marinara sauce started for our dinner, we sat down and began to do our usual check in. Jenny told us that she and Sam had started to deal with their sexual issues in their couples' counseling. "I have to give him credit for trying. He wants to make our marriage work," she related. "It may be too far gone, but we both have a lot invested. Our love life is pretty much nonexistent at this point."

"I'd like to talk more about sex with all of you," Jenny continued. "I'm a mess in this arena and I know a lot of other women in the same boat. It seems like a lot of us have either no interest in sex and our husbands are climbing the walls, or we have interest but we don't know how to get what we want from the partners we're with."

"The timing is right for me," said Lena, sipping her glass of red wine. "I just started dating a new guy who's pretty interesting. He doesn't fit into either of my usual 'bad boy' or 'nice guy' categories. I met him at a travel bookstore right before I went to the Yucatan. We were both checking out the guide-books. He owns a hotel in Costa Rica. He brings people down from this country to participate in a Spanish language program. So he goes back and forth a lot. He's a widower in his mid-50s and *very* handsome."

Much hooting and howling erupted in the group at this revelation.

"Ooo Lena!"

"You go girl!"

"We haven't made love yet, but it could happen any time. There's a lot of energy between us," she continued, blushing. "I'd like to get it right this time, but I feel really nervous."

Chatting about the predicaments of women's sexuality, we dove into a hearty dinner of spaghetti, salad and garlic bread. "I don't think I've ever sat around and talked about sex with a group of women," said Sophie, grabbing another piece of bread from the basket.

"From my experience, even though women's magazines are full of advice about sex, real dialogue doesn't happen often," I commented. "There seems to be a tremendous taboo against it. I've been in groups of outspoken women so often over the years, and yet sexuality rarely gets discussed. But I think many of us struggle with different aspects of our sexuality at times, and it would be very helpful to talk to other women about it. I'm curious how the rest of you besides Jenny and Lena feel about this issue?"

"Who has the energy for sex?" Alex threw up her hands in exasperation. "Between my kids and my work, I'm totally exhausted at the end of the day. Danny and I used to have great sex before we had kids, but we've kind of lost the thread. I just don't feel very sexual these days. It's a source of tension in my marriage, for sure. I feel bad about it, kind of guilty that I'm not being a good wife."

"Michael and I have had a good sex life," Sophie offered.

"It seems to get better over time. I heard somewhere that sex gets better as you get older and I think that's true. We didn't have that great sex when we were first together, but we've really learned how to please each other along the way. But lately, I've wanted to make love with him more than he does with me. He's taking an antidepressant medication that has reduced his sex drive. I'm feeling pretty frustrated these days."

"You and me both, honey. Obviously I haven't been sexual since Hugh died," said Elinor. "We didn't have that much sex in the last few years since his illness began either, but it was great before that. When I think back over my life, I remember my sexuality waxing and waning in phases. It hasn't been a constant. There were times when it was great and times when it was absent. I agree with Sophie though. I didn't feel like I could ask for what I wanted until I got older. It's a funny thing, when you're young you have all this raw unrefined passion and not much know how. When you get older, it seems to get reversed."

"That sounds like me and Billy," Allison said thoughtfully. "We have a lot of passion. We make love a lot. But I'm embarrassed to admit that I've never had an orgasm. I feel like I'm not a 'real woman' somehow."

"I just read somewhere that Marilyn Monroe never had an orgasm in her entire life," I mentioned. "Isn't that tragic? Here's a woman that we think of as a sex goddess who couldn't have an orgasm."

"I'm pretty limited in my sexual experience," confessed Sylvia. "When I was in college I seemed to be the only woman left who hadn't lost her virginity. I felt tremendous pressure to have sex. I went out on dates but kept fending the guys off. Finally I got drunk with this guy and we started messing around. I wanted to stop after a while, but he refused and just kept on going. It got pretty ugly. I guess you could say I was date-raped. Since then, I've really avoided my body and my sexuality for the most part. It's a big blank spot. I think I still have a lot of unresolved issues about sexuality. "

"Well, no kidding. That's a terrible story, Sylvia," said Sophie. "I'm so sorry that you had to go through that."

"Well, girls, clearly we've got some work to do here," observed Elinor.

After clearing away the remains of our feast, we decided to continue our discussion while we gave each other beauty treatments. Spreading out towels, we got into the array of massage oils, facial moisturizers, clay treatments, nail polish and lotions that different women had brought. Lena put on some music, and we settled in for an evening of play and good talk.

☀Fierce Beauty Tip

Create a sexual lifeline—a written chronology of your sexual history. Note your beginnings, your high points and your low points. Mark your sexual milestones, the key events that affected your relationship with your sexuality.

Old Wounds and Sexual Beginnings

American women have a significantly high rate of sexual dysfunction. According to a recent survey done by the University of Chicago, a whopping one-third of all women in this country have no interest in sex. Twenty-six percent don't have orgasms, 23 percent do not experience pleasure during lovemaking and 43 percent have one or more persistent problems with their sexuality. I was deeply disturbed when I first encountered these statistics. It seemed a sad statement about the collective female psyche that so many of us have misplaced our connection with what should be a natural function of our bodies and our relationships.

I grew up riding the crest of the wave of the sexual revolution.

That, in combination with a consuming need for affection and recognition from men, led me into an early promiscuity. I started making out with boys when I was 13 and lost my virginity two years later. Never wanting sex without love, I had a number of relationships with men whom I thought I loved, because we had had sex. As a teenager, in the absence of any supervision or guidance on the home front, I pretty much did what I wanted, with whomever I wanted to do it with. I ran wild on the streets of Chicago at night, going to exotic Dionysian parties and dating all kinds of men.

It wasn't until later in my life that I became aware that in certain ways I had damaged myself through these experiences. My desperate need to be loved, the lack of a strong safe family container, and perhaps the wave of collective sexual experimentation that was woven into the fabric of that time, drowned out the voice of a vulnerable young girl who needed something quite different for her sexuality to thrive.

When, at the age of 30, I began to more deeply explore who I was as a sexual being, I discovered that there was a part of me that was actually still only about 13 years old. She was standing at the edge of her sexuality, fearful of the unknown, delicate in sensibilities and extraordinarily vulnerable. No sexual partner had ever touched that young girl on any level. I realized that my sexuality was like a fragile flower that had been trampled upon and therefore had never truly blossomed. At that time in my life, I often fantasized that I lived in a sacred place such as a temple or some other cloistered environment. Instinctively, I longed for my sexuality to be held in the context of soul.

Up until that time, although I had experienced a great deal of passion and many sexual escapades, I had actually known very little real pleasure in my body. In fact, my body was largely invisible to me. I walked around in it, but didn't have a clue about its many possibilities as an instrument of pleasure and sensuality. Soon thereafter, however, I began to get regular massages from an older man, whose touch delighted me. For the first time in my life, my body sang. For me this was the beginning of the budding of my true sexuality.

When I look back over my life and the times that I grew up in, it seems that the sexual revolution had very mixed benefits. Certainly, the freedom it championed opened doors for many of us to experiment with our sexuality. We discovered facets that we may have never otherwise known. On the other hand, all this opportunity for a variety of experience does not appear to have brought women to a higher degree of fulfillment sexually. In fact, for many women, it has had negative consequences, both to their bodies and their hearts. Many of us are still looking for the right set of rules to live by.

Because our sexuality can become obscured or constricted by damaging early experiences, the Fierce Beauties decided to explore the significant events and belief systems in our lives that were the foundations for our current sexual identity. Once we cleared these obstructions out of the road, we could more easily move forward with a design more of our own making.

I queried the group who were by now in various prone positions with light green face clay crustily adorning their faces. "How did we become who we are sexually? Where did we lose parts of ourselves or take in beliefs that were destructive?"

"I remember my mother yelling at me and my friend Toby when we were about five years old," Sylvia mused. "We were playing in the backyard in one of those little wading pools. We took our bathing suits off and were checking out each other's tushes. She saw us and had a total fit. She started screaming about being us being 'disgusting little animals.' She hauled us out of the pool, sent me to my room, and called Toby's mother to come get him. I remember feeling really dirty and ashamed of myself. Even now I still feel the sensation of badness in my body."

"I can sure relate to that feeling," agreed Lena, nodding vigorously, despite her clay mask. "In my culture, a woman's virginity is extremely important to her family. If she loses it before marriage, like I did, she brings dishonor onto her family's name. I was actually having a pretty good time with my high-school boyfriend. He really cared for me. We were very sweet together, but our families just blasted the whole thing apart. It took years for my father to forgive me."

"The biggest sexual milestone for me was having kids," reported Alex. "My sexuality just disappeared. My breasts were there for nursing not lovemaking. I felt overwhelmed by the constant physical contact I had with my kids crawling all over me. At night, I just wanted to be left alone. They're a little older now, but Danny and I are still having trouble reconnecting. I don't know where it went and how to find it again."

"In the beginning my husband was very uncomfortable with any kind of sexual contact other than the usual 'missionary' position with him on top," contributed Elinor. "Of course that was a long time ago and we didn't have near the amount of information that people have nowadays. I was very young and just went along with his preferences. I think he was actually somewhat repulsed by my genitals. I began to think that part of me was really ugly. Years later, all that wonderful vaginal art came out, like Judy Chicago's and Georgia O'Keeffe's, and I started to feel differently."

☀ Fierce Beauty Tip

Make a list of the sexual beliefs and attitudes of the key people in your life. Make a list of your own beliefs and compare them. What are your taboos? What do you like or not like about your sexuality?

Re-Virgining Ourselves

As contemporary women, we are the inheritors of various confused and paradoxical ideas about female sexuality. In many cases, we have internalized the legacy of these culture wars in our bodies, unconsciously learning to regard our own sexuality with fear and suspicion. Women often feel that they must choose between conflicting roles: chaste Madonnas or wanton whores, finding little permission and support to integrate both.

In addition, there are large numbers of women in our society who have had their sexuality violated through rape or sexual molestation. The pervasive threat of sexual aggression causes many young girls to feel that they have to armor their bodies and inhibit their budding sexuality as it begins to flower. They fear that if they allow themselves to completely embody and celebrate their female sexuality, they may not be able to control their effect on the men they encounter.

The cultural atmosphere around women's sexuality has been inimical for so long that collectively many women have consciously or unconsciously hidden their true sexual selves. And in some cases we've hidden our erotic soul so well that we have a hard time relocating it. Many of us have become somewhat like domesticated animals that have lost their natural wildness. From the enclosures of our contained and hampered spirits, we lift our noses to the wind hoping for a whisper, a touch, a memory, that will take us back to an unfettered and easy passion.

After becoming conscious of what we may have lost or inadequately tended, we have the opportunity to recreate our sexual unfolding in a more conscious and tender manner. In *Women's Bodies, Women's Wisdom,* Dr. Christiane Northrup suggests we all need to become virgins again, approaching our sexuality anew with unsullied tenderness and innocence.

"I feel like in order to resurrect something I need to somehow get rid of all the crap I've swallowed over the years," pronounced Sylvia. "I feel like I want to symbolically wash it away somehow. We've all got something—some hurt or fear, or bad experience. I have a friend who was raped and it completely destroyed her capacity to have sexual pleasure. It was really tragic then and it's still stuck in her now. I would hate to think that we couldn't release these things and move on."

We spontaneously decided to enact a simple cleansing ritual. We wrote down all the junk, all the hindering and repressive messages and hurtful sexual experiences we had received from parents, religions, peers and partners. Then we crowded into Sylvia's bathroom and one by one, tore up our papers and flushed them down the toilet, cheering as the last remaining bits swirled and disappeared.

"That was great. I feel better," announced Allison, with a sigh of relief, as we traipsed back to the other room. "It seems ridiculous, but I do."

"Me too," agreed Lena. "I'm ready to re-virgin myself now."

Rituals like these do not magically remove past traumas, but they do act upon the psyche, signaling a readiness to move on and take in new information. If the trauma goes deep and is pervasive, different therapies and bodywork interventions can be necessary to support healing. It is important, however, to draw a metaphorical line in the sand, and powerfully declare our intention to reclaim our erotic potential.

☀ Fierce Beauty Tip

Explore your sexual self. How old are you as a sexual being? What kind of environment do you need to fully flower as a sexual woman? Imagine yourself in this environment. Notice the ambiance, is it wild or quiet? What are you wearing? What kind of partner, if any, do you have? What do you desire?

Breaking Down False Myths

As the Fierce Beauty Club began to reconstruct and re-own our sexuality, it was useful to replace some of the false information that we'd come to accept as fact with a more accurate picture of female sexuality. Various researchers have discovered that human beings are sexual from the very beginning of their lives.

In utero, male babies have erections and girl babies lubricate vaginally at cyclical intervals. This cyclical sexual pulsation continues in newborns. Sexuality in infants and small children is also a normal and common occurrence. In fact, in some cultures around the world, women stroke their baby's genitals in order to soothe them. Anyone who has been around small children knows that, if given the freedom to do so, babies love to play with their genitals.

This innate sexual responsiveness continues throughout childhood. Most sexual researchers and child development experts now believe that latency, as Freud imagined it—a period of prepubescent sexual slumber—does not actually happen. Many children masturbate and have sexual curiosity throughout that period of their lives.

As adults, there is a widespread belief that women are not as sexual as men. Anthropologist Helen Fisher calls this sexual fallacy the "mismeasure of women's libido" She reports that while women do not fantasize as much as men about sex, they have longer and more intense orgasms. They are also capable of more frequent orgasms. She says, "The mismeasure of women's libido becomes even more apparent if the definition of sexual activity is expanded to include sensuality . . . women's sex drive is simply different than men's, more subtle, more complex, and much more misunderstood." In fact, like men who get erections regularly during sleep, women's vaginas have a cyclical lubrication every 15 minutes. But because this is less visible, it wasn't until recently that this parallel phenomenon was documented.

Anthropologist Sarah Blaffer Hrdy extensively studied female sexuality in primates and humans. Also refuting the myth of the sexless and passive female, she observed that female primates are an assertive and horny bunch. She concluded, "Women have been biologically endowed with a lusty primate sensuality."

Not only does misinformation abound, there is also a general lack of good information about women's sexuality. It wasn't until I was in my early 30s that I discovered that I became more interested in sex when I ovulated. The biological mandate to conceive produces a sexual quickening. This bit of information would have been important to know when I was a teenager first engaging in sex. How many women, riding the roller coaster of ovulatory lust, have chosen the nearest available man, disdaining birth control and abandoning all reason?

Many of us have been held by the sway of the "myth of the vaginal orgasm." This particularly destructive fantasy has caused many women to feel inadequate sexually. In fact, as many as 70 percent of all women do not have vaginal orgasms. It is now believed that the clitoris needs to be within a certain close proximity to the vagina to be stimulated to orgasm during intercourse. So if your clitoris is situated further back, as most women's are, you're out of luck. This information should ideally be conveyed to young girls when they first become interested in sex. Otherwise, many women spend years wondering what they are missing and why they are not responding as expected.

What *is* true is that women, just like their physical apparatus, are complex sexually. Women's sexuality could be imagined as a gate that is shrouded by a number of veils. To go through the gateway, we have to part each of the veils. The sexual revolution may only have parted the first one or two of the veils, leaving the rest still to be revealed. In her book *Woman*, Natalie Angier reminds us that, "A woman's sex drive is an involved instrument. It is tied to mood, mentation, past experience, the Furies. At the eye of the storm is the clitoris. The clitoris is our magic cape. It tells us that joy is serious business and that we must not take our light, our sexual brilliance lightly."

Another reason that sexuality is complicated for heterosexual women is that it is difficult for them to separate their sexuality from the possibility of pregnancy. They are closely woven together physically and emotionally. Whenever we make love we risk pregnancy, regardless of birth control advances. Certainly this is also true for men, but the consequences for women, their bodies, and their emotional and physical health are far more immediate and significant. Until recently, women frequently died in childbirth. Sex, for women, therefore, could be not only life changing but also potentially life threatening.

Parting the veils of women's sexuality comes about largely through opening previously closed lines of communication. In *The Erotic Silence of the American Wife*, Dalma Heyn writes, "With no expression of a girl's erotic feelings, no discourse of pleasure and desire passed from mother to daughter, no narratives of a girl's coming into sexual awareness, there exists no language for them in which to speak about their experience." Mothers need to talk to their daughters; daughters need to talk to their girlfriends; friends need to reach out to other friends; and lovers need to talk to lovers. In this way we begin to piece together the missing erotic heritage, gone so long from the Motherline.

☀Fierce Beauty Tip

Get together with a close and trusted woman friend and share some of the intimate details of your sexual experiences. Compare key events, such as first sexual experiences, best and worst sex and most exotic. Have fun and learn from each other.

Finding Our Erotic Voices

It was getting late and a few people were feeling sleepy. We spread out our pillows, quilts and sleeping bags on Sylvia's living room floor. Lena set up the VCR in preparation for watching a movie. Allison, dressed in oversized pink t-shirt, helped me make some popcorn. We sprinkled Parmesan cheese and a touch of cayenne on the popcorn and put it in several bowls.

"I was relieved to hear that I wasn't a weirdo for not having orgasms with Billy," she confided. "I thought there was something wrong with me. But it occurs to me that I have never really told him what I wanted, I'm not even sure that I know. And talking about it is so hard to do. I haven't wanted to embarrass him."

Finding the language to articulate our sexual desires is difficult for many women. Speaking about sex to our partners can be a powerful taboo to overcome. It requires that we openly declare what we want. Many of us not only get lost in the emotional dynamics of our relationships, we also can get lost while making love. We are so tuned in to what other people are feeling and needing that we often cannot even feel our own bodies. If we can't feel, however, we cannot respond. Knowing what we want as women means becoming, at least temporarily, self-centered. We need to live completely inside our own skins.

Women may be just as sexual as men but men often express their sexuality with a very different style. They often get excited more readily and quickly than women. Their excitement can drown out the more tentative, sometimes quieter thread of a woman's awakening to sexual passion. It is therefore helpful for women to explore their own sexual style before they attempt to bring it to their partners. Through masturbation, better described as "self-pleasuring" we can discover where and how we like to be touched. We can allow our fantasies to develop, discovering our unique sexual language. If we don't speak it, how can anyone else?

In her delightful book *Unleashing the Sex Goddess in Every Woman*, Olivia St. Claire tells women that, "Your body is the divine instrument of pleasures fit for the gods. And before you can use it to make beautiful music with your partner, you have to become a virtuoso on your own Stradivarius. In order to seduce others with your heavenly melodies, you must first seduce yourself by drawing out your deep, wild sexuality."

There are many reasons why our sexual relationships get derailed. Sometimes relationship dynamics that inhibit the flow of energy between two people need to be addressed. But the first place to focus is always on ourselves through making an in-depth study of our own inner erotic goddess. Anaïs Nin reminds us that there is tremendous possibility in female sexuality: "The true liberation of eroticism lies in accepting the fact that there are a million facets to it, a million forms of eroticism, a million objects of it, situations, atmospheres, and variations. We have first of all to dispense with guilt concerning its expansion, then remain open to its surprises."

☀ Fierce Beauty Tip

Spend some quality erotic time with yourself. Take a warm scented bath; rub your body with fragrant oils. Touch your self with gentleness and love. How much can you let your body feel? There is no upper limit.

Fierce Beauty Girl Talk

After watching *Dirty Dancing* together, Alex, Elinor and Sylvia went to bed. Jenny, Sophie, Lena, Allison and I were still wide-awake. We curled up together in a corner, whispering about the movie.

"I love the part when they dance and he takes off her clothes while they're dancing," Lena said. "It's *so* sexy."

"No kidding," I agreed. "I can't believe how many times I've seen that movie. My daughter, Noelani, and I used to watch it together. We'd go nuts when that part came on."

"This new guy, Eduardo, and I have been going dancing a lot," Lena shared. "It's a great way to get to know somebody. A lot of relationship issues come up when you dance. You have to agree who's going to lead and who's going to follow. You have to communicate through your body language. You can't be too stiff or too fluid. You have to strike a balance right in the middle. I've decided that I want to really get to know this guy before I go to bed with him, which is a new pattern for me. I want him to learn how to part my veils."

"I think that sexuality itself is a dance," said Sophie. "It involves the whole body. Part of the problem in our culture is that we get so focused on our genitals, we can forget the wonderful body movements that can happen. When I make love with Michael, there are moments when time stops. I feel like I'm slowly moving in water and that all my cells are awake and alive. Energy flows back and forth between us. There's no trying to get anywhere, we're just in this beautiful place that is full of love and pleasure. I find myself crying sometimes when we touch this place. There's so much beauty. I think sometimes people get so focused on the goal of orgasm, we forget to be with the pleasure in the moment."

"Wow," said Allison, her eyes open wide. "I have a lot to learn."

"We all do," Sophie said gently. "There are layers and layers of sexual possibility available to be explored. Michael and I took some classes on East Indian Tantra, a sacred sexual practice. We knew some couples that learned a Native American form of Tantric teaching called Quodoshka. It opened my eyes to what a narrow band of sexuality is practiced in most of our culture. We learned about the various different kinds of orgasms that a person can have as well as techniques to enhance how much sexual energy flows through your body.

"You know," she continued thoughtfully. "I never really thought about it, but when I go out and dance in the wind on my land, I feel like an erotic goddess. I let her move in my body. That probably helps my lovemaking with Michael."

"I'm a long ways from that," Jenny told us. "The counselor told me and Sam to not even attempt to have sex right now.

She says we need to start over. She wants us to court, like we did in the very beginning. She especially wants us to play together for starters. Just have fun. It's hard for us to do. We easily get involved in talking about the kids or what the house needs, or his pressures at work. But I'm inspired to connect more with my own sexuality. Since we started talking about beauty and sensuality, I've been paying more attention to my body. I went shopping for some new clothes. See," she unwrapped her bathrobe to show us a lovely mauve satin nightgown edged with delicate ecru lace. "I'm experimenting with a new look, I love how this satin feels on my skin."

"It's beautiful, Jenny, I bet Sam will love it," said Allison.

"He probably will, when the right moment comes. But for now, it's just for me," she responded.

"And then again," she got up, threw off her robe, hitched her nightie seductively, and did an impromptu bump and grind, "I may put on some high heels, and my black boa, and knock his socks off." Then she collapsed into the bedding in a fit of giggles and we all started to laugh uncontrollably. There were some disgruntled groans from the sleeping bodies nearby.

Red-faced, with tears streaming down her checks, Lena sputtered in a whisper, "Girl, I didn't know you had it in you."

☀️Fierce Beauty Tip

What is your ultimate sexual fantasy? Write an erotic story that describes this fantasy in uncensored, graphic and sexy detail. What kind of sexual adventure would you like to enjoy? If you have a romantic partner, share your story and see what happens.

Searching for the Beloved

I woke up the next morning to the angelic sounds of the stereo playing a women's choral group singing Gregorian chants.

Elinor was quietly doing yoga in a corner while Sophie sketched on a pad with a piece of charcoal. Gradually, the others emerged from their cocooned nests of blankets. I could smell coffee brewing and the scent of something delicious baking.

We lingered over breakfast as if we were reluctant to break the spell and return to our lives. As we ate warm blueberry muffins, Allison said, "I had the greatest dream last night."

"Uh oh, here it comes," teased Lena.

"You mean you guys actually went to sleep at some point?" asked Alex, grumpily.

"Hey, you missed out," Ali replied, with a grin. "Jenny did the wild thing."

"Anyway," she continued, "I dreamt that Billy and I were making love in this beautiful place. It was a meadow with wildflowers and birds singing. There was soft grass beneath us. The way he touched me was so sweet. I'm not particularly religious, but it felt spiritual, almost as if I was connecting with God. I don't usually remember my dreams but this one was especially vivid. I've been thinking about it since I woke up. I think that spiritual feeling has been missing in our sex life."

In *The Soul of Sex*, Thomas Moore imagines lovemaking as a ritual to evoke the numinous presence of the divine. If we do not tend to the sacred, if we do not honor soul, then sexuality loses its magic, its restorative value and ultimately its pleasure as well. We may engage in sex as one body surface bumping against another surface, but we often feel empty and frustrated in the aftermath. The soul that animates our body goes untended and unseen. Sexuality without soul is like eating fast food. The advertisement looks good, but the actual meal is very unfulfilling.

Sexual repression and sexual obsession are two faces of the loss of sacred sexuality. In the first, we painfully deny the most basic affirmation of life, cutting off the bridge to a deep knowing of our lovers, as well as ourselves. In the second, we engage in an endless round of soulless sex, hoping and searching for some quality of pleasure or connection that continuously eludes us.

Sexual dysfunction in many forms, be it loss of desire, difficulty lubricating, or achieving orgasms, can come from inadequately tending our sexual experiences as sacred rituals. Our bodies instinctively know when our souls are not being honored. They rebel by shutting down or feeling discomfort. There is often an inherent wisdom in the elusive, mercurial nature of our sexuality.

Because sexuality in our culture has so long been excluded from what we consider holy or sacred, few of us know how to touch those places in each other with any consistency. If we're lucky, we have the good fortune to have lovers who spontaneously evoke the soul and the divine in our lovemaking. But for many people, this experience is rare. The sexual breakthroughs of the last 30 years have improved our understanding of the physical mechanics of sexuality but not of the spiritual and emotional dimensions.

New "rules" or codes of morality that attempt to recodify the wildness and variety of human sexuality into constricting boxes are not the answer to our contemporary sexual predicaments. Nor is a soulless and heartless journey into merely physical sexuality that ignores its power to affect us deeply. The Fierce Beauties decided that a secret to enhancing women's sexuality, to the parting of our veils, was to restore sacredness to sexuality. Through approaching sex as a ceremony, we would create the kind of container that hosts the deepest, tenderest, most vulnerable and most passionate parts of us.

Sacred sexuality does not necessarily mean deep, timeless, quiet, sensitive sex. It can also evoke the baudy goddess, who is earthy, crude, lewd, and wants, as Bonnie Raitt sings, "a man that can rock me, rock me to the bone." Sacred sexuality can evoke the wild goddess, who howls like a wolf, calling forth her animal ancestors as she rides the wild wave of her passion. There are many kinds of erotic goddesses, but they are all faces of the divine.

Opening to sacred sexuality means facing our fears of intimacy. Our secular, habitual sexual practices can provide us with safe places to hide. While we may long for something deeper, we may also simultaneously resist it. Soul sexuality has the potential to provoke deep transformation. It can break down the walls of the tower we may have created, while we waited, like Rapunzel, to let down our hair for the prince. Deep opening and connection with ecstasy and mystical union only happens when we surrender completely to sensuality and feeling.

☀ Fierce Beauty Tip

Design a sacred lovemaking ceremony with your lover. Create ambiance with incense, flowers, music and candles. Create the temple in which your bodies will be the altar. As you make love, touch each other with reverence, inviting your divine essence to be present. Following the river of passion, surrender to the flow.

Becoming Erotic Goddesses

Over our next few meetings we continued to talk about sex. Once we got over any initial hesitations, the floodgates opened. Different people brought in examples of women's erotic writing, and we shared some of our own. We talked about our fantasies and our fears. We were all trying to find ways to apply what we were learning.

"I have gotten so much out of our discussions," Allison said, warmly. "I feel very privileged, actually, to be learning some of this stuff sooner rather than later. I'm working on getting the courage to talk to Billy about the orgasm thing. In the meantime, I'm practicing on my own violin."

"I can't believe I'm hearing this come out of your mouth," said Lena, pretending to be shocked.

Alex told us that she and her husband had found some childcare and gone away for a weekend together: "We knew that our marriage was suffering because we weren't making love. It was mostly my fault. I was avoiding Danny. He also lacked a certain finesse in his approach. The idea of creating a ritual context really helped me figure out how to transition from being mom into being a sexual woman, something I was having trouble with. We stayed at a hotel on the ocean. I needed to be away from the kids for a little while to reconnect with the erotic side of myself. We just took our time and played. We made great love together.

"I don't want to lose this erotic, sensual part of me again," Alex declared. "I had gotten so consumed with work, that I forgot how to play and enjoy life. Taking this time with Danny was deeply nourishing to both of us."

"I had to spend some time grieving about what I lost around my sexuality. But now I'm enjoying waking it up," shared Sylvia. "I like the idea of figuring out what age you really are sexually. I think I'm only about 12 years old. I've been tuning into how a 12-year-old feels and responds to the world. I have a sense of what she needs now and how to give it to her. She's very shy and sensitive, and not really ready for a partner quite yet. I'm just starting to notice who and what turns me on and how that feels in my body. It's a whole new adventure. I think I've always felt so deluged by the blatant overt sexuality in the media and the people around me that I got kind of lost. My sexuality is quieter, more subtle."

"I've been challenged to use this material by myself," Sophie said, wryly. "Michael's just not very accessible right now. But I'm inspired to continue to have an erotic life anyway. We shouldn't need another person to feel alive, sexy and beautiful. I realized his lack of availability was so hard because making love with him was a sacred experience for me. I did feel like I touched God when we made love. But I'm also inspired to find that kind of communion on my own."

"You all are not going to believe what I did," said Elinor, looking around at the group with a wicked grin. "I was dancing with this guy at the rec center the other night. He's also widowed. We were having such a great time that I ended up spending the night with him. It must have been all this talk about sex. We had a great time. People think older folks are a bunch of dried up fruit, but that's just not true. It was very spontaneous. We just really fit together sexually. I don't know if that fits into the category of sacred sex, but it sure was fun. Some kind of wild goddess must have gotten activated in me. I've never done anything like that before. I don't know that anything more will come of it, but it doesn't really matter. He gave me a wonderful gift. What about you, Lena? What's happening with this mysterious Latin lover of yours?"

"Well, I'd like to tell you that I'm having mad, passionate sex like some of us around here," answered Lena. "But, I've decided to really get to know the guy first. And he's willing to do that. He's not pressuring me at all. He respects me, which is a novel experience for me. I feel a lot with him. That scares the hell out of me. But I'm trying to stay with my feelings and let myself be vulnerable without shutting it down. It's not easy. We've started making out some, which I *highly* recommend. Making out is the greatest."

"I totally agree with that," Jenny chimed in. "Sam took me out to a really nice restaurant the other night. I got all dressed up in this new outfit that Lena helped me pick out. Then we went and sat out under the stars and necked like teenagers. It was very sweet and tender. And we talked a lot, really talked. I told him about this idea of discovering the virginal places in our relationship after all our years together. I feel hopeful for the first time in a long time."

The Fierce Beauty Club had made a good start toward discovering a new relationship with our sexuality and sensuality.

Each one of us in our own unique manner had invited sacred sensuality to be a part of her life. The erotic goddesses, lost for so many years, were making a lively comeback in the Fierce Beauties. As I listened to the women talking and laughing, I could feel a growing sense of ease in our souls and in our female bodies. I was reminded of the last line of a prayer to the feminine soul that I sometimes say, which ends with the words, "There is room for you here." I thought, yes, indeed, there is room for us here in all our erotic glory and multiplicity, our wildness and our vulnerability, our joy and our pleasure.

. . .

STEP 6: Awaken and celebrate your sacred sexuality.

CHAPTER 7

Discovering Our Creative Fire

*Creativity is foremost being in the world soulfully,
for the only thing we truly make, whether in the
arts, in culture, or at home, is soul.*

—Thomas Moore

"HOW IS your transition going from being an accountant to becoming an artist?" I asked Sophie, as she showed us her latest work: a vibrant and colorful eight-foot-high painting of a woman and a man cavorting in the sea.

"Very slowly," she replied. "It hasn't been easy. I've been the primary support for our family with my accounting clients. Michael started a business creating Web sites for people on the Internet. But it's taking longer than we thought to get it off the ground. So I've had to keep some of my clients. Lately, though, doing accounting just makes me miserable. I get horrible headaches that seem to go away when I paint. We're really struggling financially. But I'm determined to make it work. I want to paint all the time. I *have* to paint," she said fiercely.

That week a local gallery displayed Sophie's art in her first one-woman show. We decided to have a potluck dinner that night at our regular weekly meeting to celebrate her success. The Fierce Beauty Club members really knocked themselves out. They set up a low table in the middle of the room that was overflowing with culinary art. Extravagant amounts of food of all sorts covered the table. Someone also placed candles, flowers and green foliage in decorative colorful designs around the dishes of food.

As we sat down around the table, Alex exclaimed, "Wow, how beautiful. This looks like a feast for the gods!"

"How about for the goddesses?" laughed Sylvia, as she playfully stuck her finger in a bowl of curry dip and licked it.

"Who made it look so lovely?" I asked, having shown up just in time for dinner to start.

"Lena was in charge," replied Elinor. "She directed us and put all the final touches on the table. It's really her genius."

Lena refused to take credit for her work, as she disentangled herself from a large apron with "Kitchen Goddess" written in bold letters across the front. "It's no big deal really, just cooking and putting out food."

"I beg to differ, Lena, you're truly an artist," Sophie argued. "I couldn't do this. My dinner capability usually peaks out at tuna fish casserole. I'm in awe of this kind of talent."

The subject of creativity became our theme for the evening. As we talked, our first discovery was that many of us, like Lena, didn't think of ourselves as being particularly creative. In my other work with women this is also a common belief. Despite the fact that some women have broken through gender barriers and received critical acclaim for their contributions to society, it is still difficult for most women to recognize and express their personal creativity. Living a creative life—a life committed to some form of passionate creative expression—eludes many women. Toward that end, there are specific strategies that women can take to increase and sustain the flow of creative passion through their lives.

Expanding Our Vision of Creativity

What do we actually mean when we use the word "creativity"? As women have entered into the creativity dialogue, commonly held definitions of creativity have begun to change. In the past, our culture generally thought of creative people as artists, writers, scientists or musicians—people who have a rare gift and have produced an expression of that gift in a public way. Creativity, to a large degree, was confirmed by public awareness and agreement. Private expressions of creativity were often ignored. We don't necessarily think of the woman who writes poetry in a personal journal or dances alone in her living room at 3 o'clock in the morning as being creative.

Our culture has also associated creativity with tangible, physical manifestations of effort, be it a painting, a symphony or a scientific discovery. Current debates on the meaning of creativity, however, are shifting to include not only a traditionally male product-oriented creativity but also a more female style of process-oriented creativity. As a result, the vast majority of female expression today and throughout history is now considered in a new light.

In the past, our traditional feminine domains were mostly private. The focus of our creative impulse was the birthing and raising of children, and nurturing the social matrix of a community. These forms of creativity lacked a definitive product, unless you consider the overall success of the human species to be one. Most men and even many women did not consider this type of "social" creativity important.

Also, traditionally women participated in collective creativity rather than individual creativity. The results of their creative efforts were more likely to be attributed to the accomplishments of their families than to themselves. The old adage, "Behind every good man, stands a woman," speaks to this phenomenon of indirect creativity.

In today's world, women have the opportunity to express their creativity in many different arenas, both publicly and privately. The urge to create is an integral part of the human experience and essential to the feminine soul. It can take *any* form. There is no limit to the possibility of creative expression available to us as women. There are creative women who manage businesses, teach school, raise children, fly airplanes, love their husbands, write poetry, sing in church choirs, cook delicious food and grow succulent vegetables in their gardens.

Clarissa Pinkola Estés speaks of creativity as the "love of something, having so much love for something—whether a person, a word, an image, an idea, the land, or humanity—that all that can be done with the overflow is to create." Creativity then becomes simply our passion for doing what we love to do. With this definition, a "creative woman" is one who follows her passion and finds a way to do what she loves. In this way, she honors something that moves from deep inside her.

The first step when a woman begins her creative journey is to examine her own belief system about creativity. It is valuable to define our own creative ground. What does being a creative woman mean to you? Do you exclude yourself from the creative life because of a narrow vision or low self-esteem? Perhaps you are already creative in a manner or an arena that you have not recognized before.

Ultimately, creativity is an intimate contract between you and your soul to uninhibitedly and courageously live the life you choose to the fullest. How do we know if we are living a creative life and honoring this sacred contract? When we can listen to the call of our passion and commit ourselves *fully* to living it out.

☀️Fierce Beauty Tip

Make a commitment to your creative process. Gather a few seeds of corn (or other kind of seeds). Holding them in the palm of your hand, think of all your creative gifts and with your breath, blow your gifts metaphorically into the seeds. Then take the seeds and bury them in the ground or fling them into an ocean or river. As you do this say out loud: "I promise to nurture and share my creative gifts."

Awakening Your Feminine Fire

When we commit to a path of individual creative expression, we start creating our own dreams instead of just habitually reacting to other people and situations. The pursuit of creativity changes our focus from dwelling on ancient wounds and current insufficiencies to a more positive and proactive attitude. We become filled with the flow of life itself wanting to be born in some unique way through us.

In Spanish and Latin American music, poetry and dance this quality is called *duende*. Duende brings a deeply passionate and intensely emotional experience of life to artistic expression. My flamenco dance teacher, Ana, used to pound her chest and exhort me to bring duende into my dance. She would stamp her feet and tell me to "Take the fire of your life and put it beneath your skirts." Poet Federico Garcia Lorca says that "duende is a power, not a work." He advises us to, "awaken the duende in the remotest mansions of the blood." When we feel our duende, we feel the power that comes from our gut—our feminine fire. Duende makes our blood throb and our eyes weep. It is a commitment to what Lorca calls the "deep song."

Duende places more emphasis on the ability to profoundly feel and express the pain and the joy of human existence than on technical mastery. It moves us beyond the constraints of our social programming to be "good girls" into the power of raw passion. When we commit fully to our passion, we are planting roots in the rich garden of our soul.

Duende is similar to the idea of "soul" in African-American culture. I sing in a gospel choir at a church in my community. Music, particularly deep song, is a very important part of the ceremony. When the singers bring their deep passion, their soul, into the music, the whole congregation is electrified with energy. The fire of the soul, as well as the love and sorrow of life are celebrated in much the same way as the duende of flamenco dance.

Creativity is our "original spark." It is that unique and highly individual mark that each woman makes upon her world. It is a connection with something that, by definition, is all her own. It is a piece of psychological ground that roots a woman in her own personal destiny in which all the disparate parts of who she is combine uniquely with her environment to create transformation. This transformation can take many forms—physical, spiritual, emotional or mental.

I challenge women to find their passion, their feminine fire. What turns you on in your life? What brings heat to your blood? What makes you quicken toward life? What do you most love? I encourage you to make a promise of commitment to follow your passion. You can create a simple ritual, preferably in the company of other women who can witness and support this important moment. This ritual consists of making a written or spoken covenant to honor your creativity in whatever form it takes and to be willing to allow the creative deep song to transform your life. Making this promise is like setting a compass to guide your course. It invites the creative voice to make its identity known.

☀ Fierce Beauty Tip

Make a list of all your current and past creative dreams. Pick the one that is the liveliest for you now. Write an invitation to this creative dream. Welcome her to come play with you. Express your willingness to make a home for her.

Identifying Your Creative Daimon

There is a deep intertwining between creativity and the path of our personal destiny. Our creative deep song—what the ancient Greeks called the *daimon*—may haunt us throughout our lives, seeking to enter our conscious awareness and influence the choices we make. In *The Soul's Code*, psychologist James

Hillman suggests that the difficult events of our early life are not merely cruel twists of fate but rather a soul-inspired preparation for our individual destiny. Creativity enters when women use the circumstances of their lives as signposts on a road moving them in the direction of a deeper calling, rather than futilely bewailing their fate. As Duke Ellington once said, "I merely took the energy it takes to pout and wrote some blues."

As we sat on pillows around the ruins of our plundered meal, Lena told us about her dream of running her own bed and breakfast hotel.

"You all know I come from a large Hispanic family. We were raised in a small apartment in Los Angeles. There were six children, my parents and my grandma all crammed into a two-bedroom place. I shared a room with my three sisters. We had a lot of love, but not a lot of space. I used to daydream about having my own room in a big house. The fantasies of this house consumed me for years. I would look at magazines and draw pictures. I'd go walk around neighborhoods and stare at the houses, imagining myself inside. I'd fix them up and furnish them in my mind.

"When I got married to my ex-husband, we rented a duplex together. It wasn't my dream house. But practical considerations won over. I never knew why this house thing was such a big deal to me. I used to dream about it almost every night. I cleaned house for other people for a while, usually resenting the hell out of them for having something I wanted.

"Then I went to school and got a degree in hotel management. I worked for a big chain for a long time. Money has been really tight, especially since my divorce. But I want to save enough money to buy into the bed and breakfast that I'm managing now. It's this big old Victorian. It has an ancient plumbing system that needs constant repair, but I totally love it. The owners and I get along really well. You know, this desire to create a home has been with me for a long time."

The next step in your creative journey is to get to know the essential or elemental nature of your creative genius—your daimon. A daimon is the spirit or the archetypal energy that flows through you, animating and inspiring your creative life. Lena's daimon was her intimate companion for years, propelling her forward to find a way to manifest her creative impulse in the world. My former teacher, Luisah Teish, used to ask her students, "Who owns your head?" She wanted us to discover what was making a claim on our soul. Once we know something about the essence of our creative passion, we can begin building a productive relationship with it.

☀Fierce Beauty Tip

To identify your daimon, think about which part of your life makes you feel most alive and most energized. This is where your passion is flowing. Is there a theme or a pattern to your particular fascination? How long has it been with you? Make a list of all the life experiences that may have influenced your passion in this arena in order to see the way that your life has hosted this daimon over time.

Geniuses at Home and Love

Home-making is one of the most common but invisible outlets for many women's creativity. This creative expression is often dismissed by many people, including women, as being merely an expression of a traditional gender role—a subservient position created by patriarchal men for the purpose of serving their needs. Unfortunately, this sociopolitical analysis reduces many women's lives to meaninglessness, taking away their sense of value and casting their life choices into an oblivion of political incorrectness.

While some women may become wives and mothers out of a lack of purpose or direction in their lives, many women choose home, relationships and parenting because their souls call them in this direction. They have a passion to nurture others and create a home. Their self-esteem often suffers, however, because our culture still does not consider tending hearth and home as a creative and valuable activity.

Traditional female activities only become prisons when we don't consciously choose them, but rather abdicate our will by following someone else's course as if it were a default program in a computer. If it is our choice to express the archetypal feminine in our role of caretaker, mother and nurturer, we can make our homes and our relationships into works of art no less worthy than a Georgia O'Keeffe painting or a Toni Morrison novel.

The woman who brings her creative passion to these activities creates a home that vibrates with life force. She stands at the center of her temple, creating a garden in which children and other family members find the necessary nurturance to flourish. Using her creative knowledge and instinct, she knows how much sunlight is needed, when to add fertilizer or transplant into larger pots. She interacts continuously with the different elements of her environment, making multiple decisions on a daily basis that require enormous creative ingenuity. No situation is ever the same; she must wield her creative insight with skill and fluid expertise.

Women know that a child grows strong when bathed in a field of love. We also know that men do the same. It is a magical and mysterious truth that is an inherent part of the intuitive and archetypal feminine creative sea in which we live. It is not our duty or obligation, but for some of us, at certain times of our lives, it is our joy, our passion and our creative choice.

"I like this idea of creative home-making," said Jenny, as we continued discussing these topics. "It makes me think about what I've done with my life in a very different way. Lately, I've been feeling so negative about 'just' being a mom and a wife. Like it didn't really count somehow because I didn't have a career like a lot of my friends. But for years, I loved what I was doing. I totally got into the mother thing. I felt like my home was like a larger version of the lap that I cradled my children in when they were small. It held my family in warmth and safety and nourished my soul at the same time."

"It gives me a different perspective on this strong desire that I have to get pregnant," added Allison. "My mother has been so negative about it I've begun to think I was some kind of sicko. I like reframing it as an act of creativity."

☀ Fierce Beauty Tip

If you think that you are not creative, perhaps there is an area of creativity in your life that you may have overlooked because your "product" is yourself or the people around you. Make a list in your Fierce Beauty journal that starts with: I am creative when I... Notice the ways that you dynamically grow yourself or others with your creative genius.

Creativity and Personal Growth

Another common creative focus for many women is their own personal transformation. Instead of directing our creativity toward an art project, our own life becomes the art project. In the flow of any woman's life, there are times when old patterns die and new ones emerge. Life is a continuous process of being born, like a butterfly emerging from the slumber of a chrysalis. We can focus deliberately and consciously on these opportunities, using our self-actualizing creative power to make the most of these changing stages of development.

This process takes a variety of skills, including focus, intuition, courage, risk-taking ability and the capacity to feel and express emotion. In her book on women's creativity, *Awakening Minerva*, Linda Firestone writes, "Transformation is moving from one reality to another...the creativity that occurs during this transformative phase enables a woman to understand, see, and imagine herself and the world differently than she did before."

These abilities are the building blocks of creative personal transformation. This art form is a woman's gift for making the life that she truly desires.

Women in touch with their feminine fire rarely get stuck in life-annihilating situations. They have the creative skill and courage to perceive what is needed and take action to move forward. They possess a fire that is unquenchable. Creative women with feminine fire find ways to use the critical events of their lives as the elements of their life art—the different colors arrayed on a palette, or the threads of a weaving. The core dramatic events of their childhood, the pain and loss of broken hearts, the threat of serious illness, all become *prima materia* for transformation.

This kind of creativity can be present especially in women whose lives have been deeply affected by some type of personal trauma, either physical or emotional. Several women whom I've worked with had the misfortune to experience life-threatening diseases. One woman, struggling with ovarian cancer, took her quest for healing and turned it into a book about her personal challenge. Her own journey subsequently inspired many other women dealing with similar high-risk diseases.

Another student, terminally ill with breast cancer, entered into an intensely painful but rewarding exploration of her psychological history, seeking to heal old wounds and clear up all of her unfinished business. The precipitating event of her cancer stimulated her emotional creativity. She was determined, in the time remaining before she died, to transform herself to the best of her ability, making her examined life her art form. This "product" would be a legacy to her 13-year-old daughter.

When a woman decides to claim her feminine fire for herself, she turns the creative feminine—an actively fecund force of nature—toward her own being. She uses her fierceness to move forward. Creatively wielding a metaphorical sword, she hacks away at the debris and muck of stuck habits, freeing her psychic, emotional and even physical space from that which no longer serves her. After the sword does its work, she brings forth her nurturing powers to sustain the growth of new parts of herself, which, like tender garden plants, need constant and gentle tending to thrive.

As we chatted about different kinds of creative expression, I asked the Fierce Beauties if there were times in their lives when they felt that their primary creativity was their own psychological process.

"Absolutely," answered Elinor, vehemently. "When I look back on the year after I broke my back, I think it was one of the most creative times of my life. It was as if nothing, including my body, worked the way it did before. The people and things that had been important to me in the past just fell away. It was like I had been hiding in my life and I couldn't hide any more. I had no energy emotionally or physically to pretend to be something I wasn't. I started telling the truth about who I was and what I wanted. The people who interested me were doing the same. I did use a sword to clear away what no longer served me. My passion for yoga was born during that time."

"My life is very focused on my own transformation right now," Jenny commented. "I don't remember any other time when there was as much upheaval going in my life. Instead of just wimping out and feeling like a victim, I am really trying to use my marital difficulties as an opportunity to work on myself. It takes a lot of will power and courage. Wasn't there a time after your accident that you just wanted to give up?" she asked Elinor.

"Oh yes, many times," Elinor replied. "It was very painful and I was terrified that I was going to be paralyzed for the rest of my life. But something in me was determined to keep going. Maybe I'm just ornery and stubborn. Or maybe I had a good dose of what Liz calls feminine fire. But all the work I did was worth it. Sometimes the worst things that happen can bring gifts. Don't you give up," she admonished Jenny, with an encouraging smile.

Fierce Beauty Tip

Making honey out of the challenges in our life is a creative art form. Think back to an event in your life that appeared to be totally negative or destructive at the time that it occurred. Perhaps you received a creative gift from the situation that you may not have recognized. Is there a current difficult situation that you can mine for its transformative gold?

Misplacing Our Creative Fire

"I envy you all. I feel like my fire's kind of fizzled out," Sylvia voiced wistfully. "I don't know where my passion is anymore. I'm 33 years old, without a husband or children. I go to work every day and spend a lot of the time in chat rooms on the Internet in the evening. My job is okay. It pays the bills and the people I work with are nice. But I'm not excited about anything.

"When I grew up, the need to be financially self-sufficient was drilled into me. So I went right through school and got a degree in business because it looked like the most lucrative way to go. I have a bank account, a health plan and good benefits. But now I feel like, so what? I'm not happy and I don't really know how to change it."

"What happens to your creative flame?" I asked Sylvia. "What's stopping the flow of creative passion in your life?"

We are all potentially creative beings with gifts to give, but sometimes the flow of passion gets dammed up or impeded in some way. We may know what our passion is calling us to do but not be able to carry it out. Or, in some cases, the daimon is so buried and obscured we cannot access it. For many women, the pressure of economic and familial responsibilities, the fear of taking risks, and inadequate support from people around them can douse their fire. When we ignore our creativity, however, it usually finds a way to get our attention. Our creative daimon will make some kind of disturbance in our psyche, such as the headaches Sophie got whenever she did her accounting work.

The resulting disharmony can take many forms. In Sylvia's case, she felt a sort of apathy or numbness. Of the one in four American women who suffer clinical depression at some point in their lives, I would bet that many of them have lost the thread of their own passion. They don't know what they want or how to get it. They may think that they hunger for more love from a man or material wealth. But, in my experience, most of these women, really crave a deep, abiding and fruitful relationship with their own creativity—the true soul food.

Ignoring our creative fire also wreaks havoc on our relationships sooner or later. We may be able to suppress it in the name of business as usual at work or at home, but eventually the fire erupts. Some women sit on their dreams and desires in order to please the people around them. They don't feel safe enough to truly be themselves. They obsess about the behaviors of the people around them because they aren't living inside themselves. A wife may focus only on supporting her husband's passions. A mother who fails to give voice to her creative yearnings will tend to project them onto her children, insisting that they follow her passions in her place.

For example, my mother was adamant that I learn to play the piano. As a small child I was given lessons and expected to practice daily. Nobody ever asked if I wanted to play the piano. My mother used to tell me how much she wished she could play and how special my musical gifts were. This was designed to make me feel guilty and practice more. I finally rebelled when I was 11 years old and saved enough babysitting money to buy my own guitar. Because my mother felt unable to follow her own desire to play the piano, she tried to live her passion out through me, leaving both of us frustrated and unhappy.

A woman who has lost or never even known her own dreams may also resent her husband's focus on his work, because she has none to call her own. Some women will, in lieu of creative outlets, become obsessive about cleaning their houses. Busy work becomes our addiction, as well as alcohol, food and other substances that fill up the void within us that is our unmet and unexpressed soul creativity. It is possible to suppress the creative life but only at great cost to the feminine soul.

☀️ Fierce Beauty Tip

Get to know your creative saboteur. What is your unique style of blocking or undermining your creative voice? What are the words you hear in your mind? How does it feel in your body? You may need to confront this part of yourself and ask her to knock it off. You have a right to express your soul dream.

Getting in Our Own Way

"When you talk about this, Liz, I actually feel fear in the pit of my stomach," said Sylvia, nervously rubbing her belly. "I don't exactly know what scares me. I'm afraid that if I go down this road, my nice, neat little world will change. Maybe I won't want to go to work every day."

She got up and started pacing around the room. "I mean, who the hell knows what could happen if I start paying attention to my soul life?"

I hear a lot of women complain about not having enough time to be creative. They say that work, their families or both demand too much of their energy. While these are very real factors that influence our time and energy, many of us are afraid to truly open the door to creativity. And this fear is not unfounded. The call of a creative life can make a significant claim upon us, changing both our internal and external realities.

Some women who are embedded in family life may need to separate, at least to some degree, from the people around them. They may want or need to have time and privacy in which to be creative. Separating out of the energetic field of the "we" that many women live in can be threatening, not only to the people around us but to ourselves. This is an opposite, though parallel, fear to the male dread of drowning and losing their "I" in intimate relationships. We each fear what is more unfamiliar to our traditional male or female modes of behavior.

Fear of separation is a very real experience for many women. We often think that if we do not constantly tend the people around us that we will be cast adrift and consigned to a life of loneliness. We may think that our worth is based upon our ability to fulfill other people's needs. This is an irrational fear, but nonetheless it inhibits our willingness to make time and space for a creative life.

We may also fear that, through paying attention to our inner landscape, we might encounter unconscious emotional contents previously suppressed. Some of us have old wounds locked in our hearts that, until they are allowed a voice, can obstruct our creativity. Like powerful dragons they lie underground, guarding the cache of jewels that is our creative passion. Honoring our creative life means feeling all our emotions more strongly.

Some women tell me that they resist focusing on their creativity because they fear that nothing will happen. They worry that they will discover that there is nothing but emptiness inside of them. They avoid confronting that possibility. We also fear that we won't be perfect. We avoid creativity because we think that nothing less than perfection is worthwhile. We are often afraid to make ourselves vulnerable to our own or another person's judgment.

The creative process is much like sailing a boat. You cast off from shore, letting go of your known, habitual world. You then put up the sails, hoping to catch a breeze. This breeze sometimes fails to come at all; in which case, you flounder around in the doldrums. At other times a good steady wind comes up, taking you exactly where you want to go. Or a wild and nearly uncontrollable gale arises, and it's all you can do to stay afloat.

When I write, I have to overcome the fear that I may get little wind and suffer the consequences of feeling unproductive and barren. Or I may become lost in a hurricane of creative force and my family's needs will get put aside for a while. But one way or another, my conscious ego has little control over the creative process. It comes from beyond my known world. Its source, direction and effects on our lives are mysterious, unpredictable and uncontrollable.

Most students of the creative process will agree that being creative, regardless of the medium, involves an element of risk. If you are a woman struggling to find your passion, it is helpful to explore your fears, especially with other like-minded women who are interested in finding the same kind of connection within themselves. Often, when we speak our fears aloud to compassionate girlfriends, they just miraculously melt away. Our inner demons seem much smaller when brought out into the light of day.

One exercise that helps in dealing with fears is to imagine your creativity as a flame. Close your eyes and imagine that flame as being located down in the center of your pelvis, right in the vicinity of your uterus. How strongly does your fire burn? Is it a small ember in danger of sputtering out? Or does it burn brightly and steadily? What do you need to tend the flame of your creative passion so that it will burn brightly? Doing this exercise on a daily basis usually has a powerful effect on a woman's ability to find the courage needed to commit herself to her creative life.

Setting Out to Sail

Over the next few months, the Fierce Beauties played with different kinds of artistic media during our meetings. We brought in clay, paints, pastels and music, and did writing and movement exercises. We practiced *allowing* creativity to move us. Without concern for what things looked like, we just wanted to know what it felt like to get our programming and egos out of the way, so that deeper voices could be heard, felt and expressed. We created an environment for each other that was safe enough so that no one felt self-conscious or criticized.

We noticed that there were times that we felt like we were really in the stream of creative flow. Certain common elements were often present during these experiences: playful and spontaneous feelings, a forgetting of the outside world, a lack of awareness of the passage of time, an effortless expenditure of energy, a feeling of wholeness with all the parts of ourselves working together, a sense of sureness and confidence, laughter, and increased levels of physical and mental energy.

Women's creative process is often similar to being pregnant and giving birth. We are certainly fertile with much more than just potential children. When first pregnant with a creative idea, we begin to host a new organism that is taking root within us. This provokes numerous changes in us on very deep levels, both physically and emotionally. We start organizing our lives to protect and nurture the fragile life within us.

Our biggest challenge is to create the space, both within and without, for our creative seed to flourish. We need to build a nest or create a womb that will protect our vulnerable and not fully matured creativity. Most of us find it difficult to set aside uninterrupted time to think freely about ideas and allow our imaginations to be at play. Boundary setting is challenging for many women. Saying no, regardless of how nicely we say it, often feels rude to women. Learning to define and sustain creative space, however, sometimes necessitates having a boundary.

For women whose daily lives are intertwined with family members, it's useful to engage the whole family, including small children, in a discussion about the importance of being creative. We all need to express ourselves creatively in order to be healthy. When families understand this concept, they can make agreements to support each other's desires for creative time. Fathers and mothers can mutually agree to not only protect their children, but their partner's soul needs as well.

On a more internal level, we can develop cooperation between different aspects of our psyche. We now believe that creativity involves both hemispheres of the brain—the intuitive, emotional right side, and the logical, more linear left side. In the same way that we need a male and a female to create a baby, we need both internal male/female aspects of ourselves to birth creative expression. If we are only accessing the female side, we may have many good ideas, but lack the capacity to sustain them through to complete fruition.

Sophie, who we affectionately called our "creativity guru," described this as an inner marriage:

"The male part protects and defends my space," she offered. "I call him my inner bouncer. He keeps the external world from intruding on me. That allows the female part of myself to remain soft and fluid, internally focused. That's the place where all my ideas come from. But this other, more focused, tough guy helps me finish the paintings and then gets me out hustling my work to gallery owners. It's a great inner partnership."

Sometimes developing their own creativity ritual can help women drop into a creative mindset. What do you need to allow deep, free, spontaneous movement in your psyche? I find it essential to be alone in quiet space. I also like to meditate before I open my computer, letting go of mundane concerns as much as possible. I offer a prayer to the place of mystery that is the source of creativity, expressing my willingness and openness to be a vehicle. Some women light candles, or put on special music. Others need to organize their physical space in a particular way or visualize their creative flame. Creating a regular routine signals your readiness to commune with your creativity to both your inner psyche as well as the world around you.

☀️Fierce Beauty Tip

Make a special creativity altar. Place objects on it that are symbols of your creativity or tools that you use to create with. Spend some time daily sitting with your altar. Use it for inspiration and as a visual reminder of your creative self.

Sustaining the Creative Life

Sustaining the creative life is not an easy task in a world that is more often focused on superficial values and material wealth. It helps to create a support system around you made up, not only of your family, but also of close women friends. As we discovered through our meetings, there is tremendous power in female community. Each member of the Fierce Beauty Club used the encouragement of the group to make a greater commitment to living out her creative passion. We each, of course, had a unique way of doing this. One night, I asked the Fierce Beauties to share how they were using the information and support of the group in their lives.

"When I started taking quiet time to make space for my dreams," Sylvia recounted, "I remembered that when I was 10 years old, my grandparents gave me an old camera. I loved taking photographs with it, but when I got into high school, my parents pressured me to put all my attention into academic pursuits.

"So recently I went out and purchased a new camera and started spending all my free time taking pictures. I even met a new male friend with similar interests while snapping photos at the local mission."

As she showed us some of her photographs of old stone architecture, she told us that she was feeling very rebellious at her job.

"I'm having fantasies about leaving work. I want to take a photography trip to Africa, and have some time to kind of reevaluate my life. I can't believe I'm thinking like this. I mean, what about my retirement plan? I do have enough money saved up to live on for a while. One part of me gets incredibly excited about doing this. The other says 'Sylvia, you've lost your marbles.' Actually, that voice sounds remarkably like my father's."

"Remember that movie *Dead Poets Society* with Robin Williams?" Elinor asked the group. "He's a teacher who exhorts his students to '*Carpe Diem*,' or 'Seize the Day.'"

"I think she's saying, 'go for it,' Sylvia," explained Lena.

"Well, I'm trying to get pregnant with my husband," announced Allison. After a flurry of excited reactions from the group she continued, "I used some of these creativity techniques to tune into myself. I wanted to make sure that this was really my own choice for my life, and not the old biological clock thing or the pressure of my parents. I spent some time down by the ocean, and came to the conclusion that I'm totally ready, willing and into becoming a mom. We've started fixing up our house and building a new room for the baby."

"Well I'm on a mission to bring yoga classes to senior citizens," Elinor announced, proudly. "I know I have something to offer. Yoga has been so helpful to me and I really enjoy teaching it to other people. It feels so right for me at this point in my life."

Lena, who had never thought of herself as creative, was working on becoming a part owner of her successful bed and breakfast inn. She had joined a special class for women in business that was helping her do some serious financial planning.

"I am able to provide a nurturing, homey atmosphere that people seem to enjoy," she reported. "Since we've been talking about creativity, I realized that I'm really good at creating a certain kind of environment. And I love doing it. It's easy for me. I guess I always had this idea that creativity was something that required enormous effort. Doing this every day feels like a blessing. I get to make a beautiful garden and cook delicious food for a living."

Alex, a sales rep for a group of women who made hand-painted silk clothing and fabric art, passed around some of her sample silk scarves. We fingered them longingly and draped them around our heads and shoulders with lust in our hearts.

"I always thought that the women that I sell for were the creative ones," she mused. "But when we started expanding our definition of creativity, I realized that I'm a very creative person too. I love to do marketing. I'm good at it. I enjoy going from store to store with my bags full of samples, like some gypsy woman with her wares. I have lots of good ideas about how to expand the business. I actually feel like I'm pregnant with quintuplets right now. The artists I sell for all hate this part of the business, and they're not very good at it. So it works out well for everyone."

Jenny spoke hesitantly, "I'm mostly just working on myself. Since my separation from Sam, my world's kind of fallen apart. But I'm really trying to use this whole experience to learn how to take care of myself in a new way. I'm taking classes at the community college and I've been going out ballroom dancing with Elinor.

"I used to love to dance when I was younger. Actually when I was a kid, I used to create dance shows with my sisters all the time and perform them for my parents. It feels good to dance again. Some part of me that died is coming alive again. I guess my creativity is all about recreating my life right now. When I was a young mother, I was happy to cherish my kids and my home. Now I'm in a new place in my life and I'm trying to meet it with everything I've got."

Creativity ebbs and flows through the different phases of our lives. What may be vital and alive for us at one time of our life may become stale at another. Living a creative soul life means making an ongoing commitment to stay tuned in to our deep intuitive voices so that we can fully embrace each new movement as it appears. The creative female psyche is in constant flux as we wax and wane through menstrual moon cycles, childbirth, menopause and elderhood. Tending the feminine soul means honoring these cycles and willingly responding to the claims they make on us.

"I've been getting some exciting ideas about my art," said Sophie, pushing her mop of red hair away from her face, which uncovered a smudge of blue paint on her forehead. "All the energy we've put into our creative process in the group has definitely had an impact on me. Remember that wind you talked about, Liz? It's picking up and blowing me to some new places. I'm starting to think about some new media for my work. I want to get even bigger with my work."

"What about you, Liz?" asked Alex. "How is your creative life unfolding?"

"I feel more focused on my creativity than ever before," I responded. "I have to say that committing to it is the most profoundly liberating thing I've ever done. I have a growing sense of ground underneath me that is not easily denied, thwarted or ignored. I no longer get so easily lost in thinking that the keys to my happiness and fulfillment are in the hands of some other person. I used to waste a lot of time and energy on that delusion. My creative life now gives me a more solid identity and a stronger sense of my priorities.

"My biggest challenge is to believe that if I pursue my creativity fully, I will still meet my financial needs. That's tough. There are days when I think I must be out of my mind to try and make a living as a writer and a teacher working outside an established institution. An old voice says, 'I should get another steady job with a retirement plan.' But, I intuitively know that I'm on the right track. Being with all of you regularly helps me to believe in my dreams.

"I notice that I've gotten much more adept at holding the threads of my creative projects while doing other things. It's not unusual for me to write, do laundry, think about what's for dinner and answer the business phone in the same time frame. I'm not one of those creative women who can focus on a project to the exclusion of other parts of and people in her life. My home and my family are very important to me. I like to take the time to tend to their well-being. But, as a result of the work we are doing together, I'm more able to find a flow that works to keep all these parts of me alive and well."

The creative life is full of limitless possibility for women. Spiritual teacher Marianne Williamson says, "The actualized woman is powerful unto herself and gives birth to things divine." Until we embrace our creativity, we live in shallow ruts, playing it safe and allowing other people's dreams to control our imaginations and our daily lives. But if we let our own duende dance us fully awake, our lives will have purpose, vitality and meaning. We will contribute to the world the true gifts that emanate from the depths of our feminine souls.

So, Go Girls! Light your fire and get in your creative boat. Raise the sails and cast off from the shore of your life. The world awaits the fruit of our fertile souls. Feel the fear and do it anyway. The wind is coming and will blow you to the only place there is to go—home to yourself.

· · ·

STEP 7: Discover and express your creative passion.

CHAPTER 8

Being in Relationships Without Losing Ourselves

When we speak of loving someone, what we mean is that that person acts as a mirror for the place within us that is love.

—Stephen Levine

THE LONG California summer with its customary blanket of fog had given way to the crisp, clear days of fall. It was now almost dark when we started our meetings. Sophie's studio was softly lit with small table lamps and candles. Everyone was there except Alex, who had missed the last two groups.

"Where's Alex?" asked Sylvia. "She hasn't been here for a while. What's going on with her, does anyone know?"

"I talked to her on the phone yesterday," said Sophie. "She said the kids have been sick, and Danny's had late meetings at work. But she was going to try to come tonight."

We chatted quietly, waiting for Alex before we began. After a short while, we heard the sound of a car on the road and a few minutes later, Alex burst into the room, looking sheepish.

"I am *so* sorry, you guys," she apologized, as she tried to catch her breath. "I'm having a really hard time getting away from the house to come to our meetings. I've started to feel guilty about taking time away from my kids at night to come here. They like it when I'm there to put them to bed." She found a place to sit on the couch next to Lena and pulled off her jacket.

"I'm incredibly frustrated," she continued, looking around at the group. "I'm trying to juggle everything and everybody and getting lost in the shuffle. I run from one person to another in my life trying to give them what they want. But then I lose myself in the process. When I'm here, with all of you, I feel connected with myself. I get clearer about who I am and what I need. But I go home, and I can't remember any of it. Do any of you have this problem?"

"I definitely do," affirmed Lena, giving Alex's hand a squeeze. "I've had every intention of being a different kind of woman in this new relationship, but I find myself slipping right back into automatically trying to please him. I don't know how to please myself and please a man at the same time."

"Things are kind of stuck with me and Billy," Allison admitted. "After all that great talking we did here about sex, I thought I would be able to make some changes in our relationship. But I'm finding it harder to do than I thought. I have a hard time knowing what I want, much less asking for it."

"That's exactly what I'm trying figure out in my life," shared Jenny, sitting up straight in her chair. "In the counseling work I'm doing with Sam, I've realized that I wanted him to love me more, but who is 'me'? If I don't know, how can he really know how to love me? I didn't have a clue before, but I'm gradually starting to have a sense of myself."

Lost in Love

A common dilemma for many women is the loss of identity they experience when dealing with other people's personalities and the complex needs of their families. Yet, most women still desire marriage or some form of long-term committed relationship. We are also, as researchers have discovered, happiest and most satisfied when we have it all—work, children and marriage. Yet, for the most part, the women that I meet in my groups and workshops seem to be struggling with this challenge: How do we sustain our individuality in the context of our relationships with others?

Some women quest for solutions to the problem and others give up. I know an increasing number of women, particularly in midlife, who feel that they cannot find a partner with whom they can be themselves. Many of them have been in marriages that ended in divorce for this very reason. They are tired of trying and have chosen a more solitary lifestyle that at least allows them the spaciousness to be who they are without hindrance or compromise. For many, though, the choice to be alone is born out of frustration and fatigue, rather than a genuine desire for solitude. In our more intimate discussions, they admit that they often struggle with an enduring loneliness.

Many capable women, actively engaged in successful careers, get into relationships where they seem to lose their voices as soon as they fall in love or have children. I know independent, highly creative women who became mothers and then found it almost impossible to feel their own inner life anymore. The capacity for relationships is both women's genius and our downfall.

"What happens to us when we get involved in intimate relationships, either as friends, lovers or parents?" I asked the group. "How do we misplace ourselves? Why do we forget the truth of who we are and what we want?"

"For me," answered Jenny, "it wasn't a question of misplacing myself. I don't think I ever knew. Sam came along when I was very young. He wanted me. It was that simple. And I so badly wanted to be wanted, I didn't even think about who he was or whether we were even compatible. I created a storybook life for myself. Sam was handsome and sure of himself. He seemed to know what he wanted, so I just went along with it."

"I think I'm actually afraid of Billy leaving me if I don't do it right," Allison said, thoughtfully, pushing her hair away from her face. "My dad divorced my mom when I was eight years old. They used to fight about me a lot, so I blamed myself. Now I find myself being very anxious to please Billy all the time."

"I can relate to that," agreed Lena. "I can be very independent when I'm alone. But when I start to care about someone, forget it. It's all over. I turn into mush. I'd do practically anything to hold onto someone that I love. It sounds terrible and I'm embarrassed to admit it, but it's true."

"But it doesn't work," argued Jenny, emphatically. "I went down that road, and look where it got me. You just can't give up yourself."

"I know women at work, though" said Sylvia, "that have gone to the other extreme. They only think about themselves in this totally self-centered way. They scheme to get rich guys who will buy them lots of expensive things. They expect to be served and catered to. I feel sorry for the guys they get involved with."

"Well, clearly we need to figure out how to be capable of honoring ourselves and the people we care about," suggested Elinor.

In the Fierce Beauty Club, we had done a great deal of work on ourselves. Our next step was to learn how to create healthy bridges between ourselves and other people. We were searching for the capacity to sustain a deep abiding connection to our own souls while fully participating in intimate relationships and careers.

☀Fierce Beauty Tip

Are there parts of your identity that you are not expressing in your family life or intimate relationship? Spend some time by yourself and notice if your energy, personal habits and forms of expression change. Spend time with other friends and notice how your personality shifts when you're with different people. Who is the real you? What are you giving up to be loved by others?

Facing Our Fears

There are various psychological and historical factors that contribute to women losing their power in their intimate relationships. Because relationships are so very important to most women, the loss of relationships is anathema. The fear of this loss often rears its ugly head when we step out of traditional passive gender roles and assert ourselves, either in communicating what we need from others or in our desires for creative and professional expression.

In addition, since the industrial revolution, when large numbers of men began to leave the home to go to work each day, many of us had absent fathers, whose attention and affection were in limited supply. As adults, we then entered relationships with an accumulated "father hunger." This hunger, to be seen and cherished by a male, can get us into all sorts of trouble. It can silence our voices, obscure our natural desires and undermine our clarity of thought. Our need to be loved can paralyze our will. We may limit our expression or change our behaviors. We fear telling the truth about ourselves, because we suspect that the truth will be unacceptable, and we will then be rejected.

Through understanding and facing our fears, women can free themselves from this dubious enchantment. When we look directly into the face of our demon—the fear of separation or being unloved—we can emerge from what, for many of us, is a miasma of confused personal boundaries and unrealistic expectations. The first step to achieving this is to become more aware of how it feels to be run by our fears instead of by our strengths. We can become more conscious of when our decisions about how to act, think and speak are influenced by our fears of separation or abandonment. This means learning to recognize when our behavior has become compulsive, needy or inauthentic. If we determine that, in fact, we are not operating from a centered place of power in a relationship, there are several specific steps we can take to restore our balance.

Learning Compassionate Detachment

Over my 15 years of marriage with Aaron, I have learned a great deal about the need for compassionate detachment. He is a man who has a cyclical need to withdraw—we call it ebbing and flowing. When he ebbs, he becomes quiet and withdrawn. He wants to think and write. In this state, he often resents any demands that I place on him for connection. He wants to retreat into what John Gray in *Men Are from Mars, Women Are from Venus* metaphorically called the "cave." If I pursue Aaron into the cave, by insisting that he relate to me, the results are usually unpleasant. He gets irritable and, if I persist, even angry; I feel rejected, and we both get hurt. Each one feels unseen and devalued by the other.

We struggled with this dynamic for several years in the early part of our relationship. For me, his withdrawal was a recapitulation of my childhood wounds. For him, my demands echoed his negative childhood experiences with a needy, invasive and overpowering mother. In the present, we came face to face with our pasts. Over the years, we both have learned how to better honor the needs of the other person, instead of always trying to change them. In my case, that meant learning to accept his need for more distance, and facing my own fears of separation. In his case, that meant accepting my needs for more consistent communication and intimacy.

There are many stories in mythology that speak to this ancient dynamic between women and men. In the Greek myth of Psyche and Eros, Psyche is married by her family to an unknown man who insists that he only make love with her under the cloak of darkness. Every night, Eros comes to her, but always before dawn he departs. For a period of time, she accepts this restriction without question. But gradually, feeling great loneliness, she begins to wonder who her mysterious lover really is. One night, egged on by her jealous sisters, she disobeys Eros. While he sleeps she lights a lantern filled with hot oil. She beholds an extraordinarily beautiful man and is so overcome with passion that she spills a drop of hot oil on his radiant body. Suddenly he awakens and flees. Psyche is left abandoned and heartbroken.

Psyche wanders in search of her husband. In the course of her restless meandering, she faces a variety of challenges or labors that she must overcome or accomplish. One of these, for example, is to sort out an impossibly large heap of different kinds of grains and seeds. Eventually, after successfully accomplishing various tasks, she is reunited with her beloved. In the process of this journey that began with separation, however, Psyche gains strength and ability. She becomes a more mature woman. She is then better equipped to engage in a more dynamic and active partnership with her lover.

This story is familiar to many women. We want to bring that which is unconscious in our relationships to light. When we try to do this, it can cause a rupture in the fabric of the relationship. Erich Neumann, author of *Amor and Psyche*, writes, "Psyche dissolves the *participation mystique* with her partner and flings herself and him into the destiny of separation that is consciousness. Love as an expression of feminine wholeness is not possible in the dark." Tasks like the sorting of seeds, are metaphors for sifting through the amorphous strands of our psyche in order to differentiate from the other people around us.

Another story about this separation/connection dynamic in relationships is the epic Hindu myth about the god Shiva and his consort, Parvati. In one tale, Shiva spends long hours sitting in meditation on the mountain. The other gods become concerned that Shiva has removed himself from the world and is neglecting his responsibilities. They send Love, known as Kamadeva, and his wife, Pleasure, to distract Shiva from his trance. At the moment that the beautiful goddess Parvati approaches, Kamadeva (who, like Eros, shoots arrows of desire) gets ready to shoot Shiva with his bow. Shiva, enraged, sends a blast of fire from his third eye, and Kamadeva is consumed in flames. As Pleasure mourns over the body of her husband, she hears a voice saying, "Your husband will return. When Shiva weds Parvati, he will give Love's body back to his soul."

Parvati, weary of Shiva's indifference and unwillingness to engage in relationship, leaves him and goes off herself to sit in contemplation on the mountain. Learning to delve into the deep green pool of life's mysteries, she becomes an accomplished spiritual teacher and practitioner. One day, a young Brahman approaches, intent on seeking her affections. She rejects him until he finally reveals to her that he is actually the Lord Shiva. Moved by his newfound desire for her, Parvati consents to marry Shiva, but only if he returns Love's body to his wife, Pleasure. Shiva agrees to do this, and, it is said, their embrace made the whole world tremble in ecstasy.

In both these stories, the heroine separates from her lover and spends a period of time tending her own soul. This detachment begins with a wounding of some kind, which is exactly the case for many of us in our relationships. We do not go willingly into the night to face our fears. Like Jenny, it can take a disruption, such as an affair, for us to begin to claim our own feminine ground in a relationship. In my case, Aaron's periodic legitimate need for space was an impetus to explore previously unknown aspects of myself and discover new sources of fulfillment.

☀Fierce Beauty Tip

The next time your partner is unable to meet your needs, instead of entering into conflict or resentment, practice compassionate detachment. Spend some time by yourself doing something you love. Call a friend and go to the movies. Take a hot bath and enjoy a juicy novel. When you reconnect later, notice how the energy between you and your partner has changed.

Feel the Fear and Do It Anyway

For many women, learning how to take the focus off their partner and return it to themselves is a tremendous act of power. It is an aikido move that changes the dynamics without entering into direct, potentially destructive conflict. Many of us spend large periods of our lives waiting and hoping for certain kinds of responses and recognition from our intimate partners. Our energy patterns are organized around eliciting these connections. If the other person is unavailable or incapable of responding the way we want, then we are diminished.

If, on the other hand, we take full responsibility for our own well-being, we can develop a self-care program that frees us from the whims and moods of others and empowers us to truly nurture ourselves in the best way possible. Not only does this act of power and self-responsibility improve the quality of our internal reality, the good results emanate from us almost magically, transmuting the psychic and emotional dynamics in our external environments.

Parvati shows us the way. She moves out of a difficult situation and takes charge of her world, redefining its balance of power. When we practice compassionate detachment at the moment we lose our ground in our relationship, we regroup. We learn first to tend our own wounds, and secondly, to fill up the empty places in our hearts. To step away from the webbing of relationship in this manner takes courage. It means becoming a "warrior of the heart" as John Welwood calls it in his book, *Journey of the Heart*.

In my relationship with Aaron, compassionate detachment meant letting go of my conviction that I could fix everything that didn't work well between us. This was difficult for me. Part of my identity as a woman was the belief that I could solve any relationship issue. It also meant that I had to recognize that there were times that the love and nurturing that I wanted was not always going to come from him. If he was not available, what were my options? I needed to find other sources of connection and support.

Over the years, I have developed a list of activities that help restore me to a place of balance whenever I lose my center of equilibrium in relationship. These include calling women friends, engaging in pleasurable activities such as hot baths, reading a good novel, listening to music or watching a television show that I enjoy. They also include different kinds of physical activities such as riding a bike, taking walks, dancing or going swimming. Sometimes I go to a movie or shopping. Through experience, I've discovered that through separating from my primary relationship and engaging in whatever I love to do on my own, I am able to soothe the parts of me that hurt and fill up the holes. I can then reengage in my relationship from a place of strength, rather than weakness.

Fierce Beauty Tip

Create a contingency plan for "bad relationship" days or nights. Make a list of good people to call and things to do that will restore your self-confidence, your faith, your humor and your larger perspective. Keep the list handy and consult it when the going gets rough.

Finding Spiritual Sources of Love

One of the most common mistakes that many of us make in our intimate relationships is to bestow unreasonable expectations on our partners. Fed by popular culture, we buy into a romantic ideal that our lovers should be our idealized perfect soul mates. From this perspective of, "Baby, Without You I Am Nothing," and "Baby, I Need Your Loving, Got to Have All Your Loving," we can believe that our lovers will be almost god-like disseminators of bliss. They should, we think, provide what is missing, complete what is unfinished and fill what is empty.

In our culture, we may place so much focus on one person filling all our needs because our kinship systems have unraveled. Women who live in extended family systems are less likely to misplace themselves in their primary relationships. They have the opportunity to have ongoing intimate connection with others. They can see themselves reflected in the mirrors of more than one person. If we see ourselves exclusively through the eyes of one other human being, there is always the possibility that our reflected image can be distorted by the particular dynamics of that one relationship.

In this condition of isolation from kinship, we also can pressure our very human partners with expectations that really should be directed to a spiritual source of "higher power." Through participating in 12-step recovery programs, such as Adult Children of Alcoholics and Al-Anon, I learned a great deal about the dynamics of codependency. Women who struggle with codependency have taken selflessness to an extreme, to the point where compassion and generosity give way to self-loss and annihilation. The natural ability that many of us have to care for others becomes codependent when, motivated by need and fear, we begin to manipulate them, instead of loving them with a generosity of the heart. An easy trap for women traditionally trained to nurture, those of us who have codependent tendencies begin to live through other people. Without a clear sense of self, we don't know where we end and another begins.

Using compassionate detachment we can discover more about what is in our own skins, face our own issues directly and learn how to connect with our own spiritual source of love and compassion—our higher power. When Shiva rejects Parvati, she redirects that desire toward a spiritual connection. Intimate relationships, while deeply rewarding sources of transformation, love and companionship, are not a replacement for a deep spiritual union with something greater than ourselves. Many people get these two different connections crossed and confused. Our spiritual needs for deep communion, love and merging with what is called "the Great Link" in the *Star Trek: Deep Space Nine* television show surpass what any one human being can provide for another. Learning how to feed ourselves in this way can free us from existing in a state of limitation or discontent.

☀ Fierce Beauty Tip

When you feel alienated or inadequately nourished by your relationship, practice connecting with the Great Link instead. Sit quietly, breathe deeply and allow your heart to expand and touch your higher power. Feel the love and connection that are available to you whenever you're in need. You are not alone.

The Power of the Bottom Line

"I was thinking when we were talking," reflected Alex, running her hand through her short blonde hair, "that the intense anger I feel sometimes is directly connected with this issue of getting lost in our relationships. I try to be there for everyone, including my clients, but eventually I get overwhelmed and start screaming at my family. Then I feel horrible afterwards. Actually, the real reason that I haven't been here lately is because

I lost it pretty badly a few weeks ago, and I've been feeling extremely guilty ever since. I've been trying to be really good to make up for it."

"That sounds like trouble waiting to happen, Alex," cautioned Sophie. "You're going to ignore your own needs for a while and then you're going to get really pissed at everybody again. The cycle will just repeat itself, if you don't get off it."

"Well, how am I supposed to do that, Sophie?" Alex argued. Her eyes glittered and her face had flushed a deep red. "You don't know what I'm dealing with here. It's easy for you to say. You don't have little kids."

The group fell into a tense silence. Lena reached over and tried to put her arm around Alex's shoulder, but Alex shrugged her off.

"Alex, I've been in a very similar place to you in my life," said Jenny. "There are some differences, I wasn't trying to run a business and raise children at the same time, which must be very difficult for you. But I'm realizing that if we don't take care of ourselves and just serve others, that we're living a lie. And a life built on a lie eventually crumbles. I can testify to that. I wonder what you really need in all this? What's your truth?"

"What do you mean, my truth?" Alex asked, defiantly.

"What's the bottom line?" Jenny answered. "When you pay attention to this conflict you're having between you and your family, what's the undeniable, inescapable thing that you realize about what you need for yourself? I've noticed that when I finally get clear what my bottom line is, there's an actual physical sensation in my body. Try it," she suggested. "Better yet, let's all try thinking about a situation that is challenging us right now. I'm sure Alex is not the only one of us who avoids focusing on herself. In that particular circumstance what do we each need and want?"

We sat together quietly for a bit. I privately reflected that Jenny seemed much stronger and clearer than I had ever seen her.

"What's true for me," began Lena," is that I'm beginning to really care about Eduardo. And that frightens me to my bones. I am afraid of surrendering my independence. I'm afraid of being vulnerable and getting hurt again."

"I had an interesting experience just now," reported Elinor, her eyes full and a bemused look on her face. "I found myself talking to Hugh, my husband who passed away last year. I told him how much I loved him, but that I also felt, for the first time, that I was finally ready to let him go. I could feel his love for me and how unshakable our bond is. But I'm ready to let someone else into my heart now."

"I'm mad at Billy," Allison confessed. "I really am. We've hit a rough patch. I hate admitting it, but it's true. I've tried to talk to him about our love life, but he just brushes me off. He won't listen to me or work anything out. I'm angry, and that scares the hell out of me."

"I think I'm definitely done with my job," said Sylvia, "I've had enough. I'm going to take this trip to Africa. I can't ignore my dreams any more.

"Yeah, Sylvia!" we cried as we all applauded her.

Alex spoke up saying: "What I think I really need is some time by myself where I'm not doing anything for anybody. I'd *really* like some time at home alone in my house, so I could be in my own environment. When I think about asking for that from my family, I feel nuts. They already feel like they don't see me enough and I always feel like an inadequate mother and wife."

Discovering the truth of how we feel about a situation or a person in our life is crucial for learning to sustain the feminine soul in our relationships. The "bottom line" is the foundation upon which all else is constructed—a place of power. It is a "felt-sense" of our own individual reality, as distinct from the realities of the people around us. We move out of the quick-sand of attempting to fulfill the expectations of others onto solid ground. The truth can be painful to face and implementing it may take courage, but doing so roots us firmly in the center of who we are.

It is very difficult, I've noticed over the years, to convince women of how essential it is to look after themselves properly. If you succeed in getting them to agree to it in theory, they find it enormously difficult to put it into practice. But one of the most significant revelations I've had regarding my intimate relationships is the degree to which my energy affects the people around me, for good or for bad. Women are often the hub of the wheel in our families. We are energically at the center of our family's emotional life. It is a powerful responsibility. We get caught in thinking that we discharge that responsibility through tending others, when, in fact, we can often do a better job by tending ourselves.

As Alex articulated so well, this can get particularly complicated for women with children. Many of us have the preconception that perfect mothering means being always there. But if we tend our own souls, then what we model for our children is a far better lesson than teaching them how to practice an out-of-proportion self-denial with all its potential accompanying symptoms of stress, depression and inappropriate anger. Better that they should not have us sometimes, and then when we are there, have us completely present with a fullness of spirit and an abundance of heart.

☀Fierce Beauty Tip

If you are a busy and engaged wife and mother, are you taking enough time to nourish your own physical and emotional health? If not, now is a great time to start making sure that your family is drinking from a well with pure water. Make the necessary arrangements to do something special just for you. When you return, notice how much better everyone feels.

Take some time to reflect on a situation that is currently challenging you. Focus on the issues and feelings that you have. Take slow, deep breaths and relax. Feel yourself sinking down into yourself. What is your bottom line, your deepest truth about the problem? Write about it in your Fierce Beauty journal.

Becoming a Warrior of the Heart

In order to implement your bottom line, it is helpful to learn how to engage in successful conflict resolution. The Fierce Beauty Club spent some time pooling our resources and gleaning from all our experiences what kinds of strategies work best for women to become warriors of the heart. To begin with, we agreed, a woman ideally would bring a certain stance to her relationships that embodied the essence of fierce beauty—a dynamic blend of femininity and ferocity. We wanted to give expression to our womanness, while being passionate about our needs for self-determination and personal expression. Becoming a warrior of the heart took skill, strategy, courage and the capacity for empathy for others.

Effective conflict resolution is a learned ability—part of what we could imagine as the art of partnership. An essential skill in any relationship, it would ideally be taught to all children as early as elementary school. Conflict resolution involves communication and listening skills, as well as assertiveness training. For couples and families, conflict is best handled by creating a structured container to hold it. When conflict permeates daily life in an uncontained manner, it easily becomes harmful to relationships and the individuals in them.

Without adequate conflict training, many of us will use a variety of methods to express anger, both overtly and covertly aggressive. In any given moment we may get enraged without thinking, taking our partner or children by surprise and putting them at a disadvantage. We may snipe sarcastically from the sidelines, or just sulk resentfully, emitting a noxious cloud of bad energy. Without proper training, displays of anger can become battles in which people are emotionally and even physically hurt. In the aftermath of this kind of mess, we can become phobic about engaging in conflict at all, choosing instead to withdraw or submerge our true feelings.

Conflict is often best handled by setting aside regular times specifically for the purpose of conflict resolution. Weekly meetings, for example, in which a couple or a family sits down together with the purpose of tending their relationships, can create a safer and more productive atmosphere for communicating issues. To do this most effectively it is helpful to implement some basic ground rules:

Before the meeting, involve each person in agreeing on the length of the session, and stick to the agreement. We all have limitations on our emotional availability.

Respect each other's expression: when one person speaks, the other listens without interruption.

Keep it balanced: each person gets an equal length of time to air his or her feelings.

Use "I" statements: talk about yourself and what you feel, rather than making observations and judgments about the other person.

End with giving appreciation for what works in the relationship and for what each values in the other.

If the conflict resolution session falls apart or becomes an unproductive battle, agree to end and try again at another time. There's nothing to be gained by participating in a war.

A basic principle of the art of partnership is the paradox that two differing people can both be right. Each person's perspective is true for them. Fruitful resolutions come when all parties feel like their point of view is valued. Most of us primarily want to be heard. We want to feel that the other person, though they may not agree with us, can at least empathize with our feelings. The capacity for "active listening," the ability to listen to another person without reacting or making them wrong, is essential for conflict resolution.

When the Fierce Beauties shared our experiences, we discovered that one of the most effective techniques to disarm potential conflict was learning how to go underneath our anger to the more vulnerable feelings of hurt that usually accompany it. We found that whomever we were angry at was usually more receptive to hearing us when our concerns were framed in a gentler manner. When we got angry about something, often it was because we had been hurt somehow.

Learning to engage in conflict in this manner requires discipline. Instead of erupting whenever we feel like it, practicing this kind of focused structure winnows out the legitimate issues in a relationship from the outbursts and irritability that result from stress. If we have concerns that we feel incapable of holding or keeping to ourselves until the conflict resolution session, we can write them down. We can record our feelings, opinions and issues and bring them to the conflict session. Slowing down the emotional process may seem contrived at first, but it actually encourages us to become more aware of our needs before taking action.

☀ Fierce Beauty Tip

After becoming aware of and accepting your truth about a particular issue, reflect on what action now needs to be taken. If communication with a particular person is necessary, arrange to meet with him or her at a time when you are both available and well rested. Standing strong on the ground of your inner wisdom, tell that person your bottom line.

Relationship as a Sacred Path

Sylvia stood up and stretched. She walked across the room to a side table where there was a pitcher of water. Pouring herself a cup, she returned to her chair. "Listening to all of you makes me understand why I've been so leery of intimate relationships. I had one encounter that lasted a little less than a year a while back. We really liked each other, but it started to get difficult at the end and we both bailed."

"Relationships are difficult," agreed Sophie. "They take a tremendous amount of work to be successful. I think a lot of people nowadays don't want to do the hard stuff. They want the goodies, but when it gets complicated, which it inevitably does, they're out of there."

Relationships can provide us with comfort, companionship and sexuality. But perhaps the ultimate purpose of intimate relationships is the making of soul. It is through our relationships that we wake up the unaware parts of ourselves, and conflict is often an integral part of that process. Some people view conflict in a relationship as an indication that there is something amiss. They have a New Age–inspired perspective that every thing should be love and light. But clashes and disagreements in relationships are a natural part of changing that often can only come about when we surrender our hearts and allow ourselves to be vulnerable to another person.

John Welwood writes, "Intimate relationships are not safe! That is not their nature. They unmask and expose us, and bring us face to face with life in all its power and mystery." He says that relationships cause us to "dance on the razor's edge" of life and encourages couples to meet this experience with willingness and courage.

Relationships can turn us inside out, confronting us with previously unknown parts of ourselves. Sometimes we find these aspects reflected back to us through our partner. In *Romancing the Shadow*, authors Connie Zweig and Steve Wolf identify this psychological phenomenon as "projection," saying, "The unconscious mind expels both positive and negative traits, attributing them to other people, whereby they can become conscious. Because, by definition, the unconscious mind is hidden, like the dark side of the moon, we need to discover indirect ways to catch glimpses of it."

Relationships, therefore, become an important vehicle for personal growth. They are mirrors that show us what we may not want, but, in fact, need to see. We are often attracted to people who display the very same characteristics that we have disowned. They are quite likely to be different in temperament. The differences between people in a relationship are both an irritant and a source of gold. Successful romantic partnerships develop through a capacity to embrace and enjoy those differences. If we allow our partners to be who they are, instead of behaving like imperialists conquering a new territory, we reap the benefits and our lives are enhanced.

The richness of diverse qualities in couples provides fertile soil for many kinds of creativity. The complementary psyches of two people give birth to a third energy. Sometimes, that union produces a child. For others, it may produce a business or an art project. Some view this cocreated energy as an intangible presence that exists in the intersubjective field between two people—the soul of the relationship. The poet Robert Bly writes:

> The man sees the way his fingers move;
> he sees her hands close around a book she hands him.

They obey a third body that they share in common.
They have made a promise to love that body.

Tending the soul of our relationships is a sacred discipline, with its own rites and rituals. When we bring this kind of depth perspective into all of our intimate connections, it provides a more meaningful context for the ups and downs of daily life. We can better understand and accept having our buttons pushed by others. In intimate relationships our hearts are broken many times. But when our heart is broken, it can grow larger. As we are moved profoundly by raw emotions, we learn how to go through the fire of pain into deep beauty and love.

☀ Fierce Beauty Tip

What is being created through the vehicle of your relationship? If you choose not to have children, or are beyond that phase of life, what is currently being born? With your partner, acknowledge this third presence that is the fruit of the soul of your relationship by lighting a candle in its honor.

Loving Others and Ourselves

Next week, Alex was uncharacteristically one of the first to arrive. With her short blond hair swinging, she seemed buoyant.

"What happened to you?" asked Sophie, as she finished cleaning up her paints and paintbrushes from the project she was working on.

"I had a meeting with my family and told them how I was feeling," Alex answered. "It was great. Everybody, even the kids, got a chance to speak. Danny offered to take them to the park every Saturday for a couple of hours. I get to stay home and do nothing. And I explained to them how important this group is to me. They really seemed to understand. So, today, I feel very encouraged. I had such a good time when they were gone on Saturday. I put on my favorite music for a change and danced. You have no idea how quickly the soundtrack of the *Lion King* can get old."

As the women gathered, Alex's mood was infectious. There was a sparkle in the air. We had felt inspired after our last meeting to look at our relationships in a different way. Over the week, we had tried on some of the ideas we had discussed.

"I got Billy to have a meeting with me too," Allison told us. "At first he was pretty uptight, but then he kind of got into it. He said that I was always trying to make him to talk to me at times when he was right in the middle of other things. It was hard for him to switch channels. He also admitted to me how pressured he feels to be the world's greatest lover, and it's hard for him to hear criticism. But I think I was able to explain how I felt in a way that didn't make him defensive."

"There's been some tension between Michael and me lately," shared Sophie, as she started what had become our ritual "tea ceremony."

"I've been wanting him to get his business together," she continued, "so I could let go of mine. I feel like it's his turn to be the main person bringing in money. But he's not very aggressive about promoting his company. I find myself getting way overinvolved. I keep pushing at him.

"I started thinking about this idea we discussed about how the shadow works in couples. I've been the one more in the world and he's been the dreamy, poetic type. He's always been good at nurturing our home and I've kept our finances together. We're the opposite of a lot of traditional couples. But I realized that instead of being mad at him for who he was that I should try and learn from him. It's given me something to think about."

Lena told us that she had felt deeply moved by a conversation that she had had with Eduardo: "I decided to just jump off the edge and tell him how fearful and vulnerable I was feeling. I admitted that I was really starting to care about him. Instead of making a beeline for the door, he told me that he felt much the same way. We talked about our past relationship failures and we ended up crying together. It blew me away. I've never had that experience with a guy before."

"That's great, Lena," said Jenny, wistfully. "It sounds delicious. I'm still working things out slowly with Sam. We're dating, but taking a lot of separate space. Sometimes I'm home alone and I don't know where he is or what he's up to. We've agreed not to see other people. But my trust is pretty low right now. One night I had kind of a panic attack, but I called Elinor and we talked for a while. Then I took a hot bath and watched some schmaltzy movie on Lifetime. Elinor suggested that when I felt really afraid I should imagine someone holding me. I tried that and it worked. I don't think I'm having nearly as much fun as some of us," she poked Lena, "but I think I'm doing some good work. What about our single ladies?"

Elinor and Sylvia looked at each other. "Well, I'll go," said Elinor. "I'm more comfortable with being by myself than I've ever been. I just don't feel like I need anyone at this point. But I am starting to date that "mystery man" that I had that "adventure" with last month. We have fun together. I don't really know if it will turn into anything serious and whatever happens is fine with me. It's liberating to feel this way."

"This is all so new to me," reported Sylvia. "I'm starting to realize the extent to which I've been hiding out from life. And I don't have anyone that I'm dating right now. But I have some new tools and a better sense of the ground underneath me. I'm being more honest with myself about my fears and my needs. I very much like the idea of thinking of relationships as a spiritual discipline. It gives me a way to deal with the intensity of relationships."

I realized that the exuberance in the room was born out of the success that we were having. Perhaps we actually could find ways to nourish ourselves as well as the people around us. The possibility of this was hopeful and exciting. An old anthropology teacher of mine once told me that the greatest source of power in the world was the ability to cross cultural lines and move freely through many different arenas. Tending our feminine souls while we go to work, take care of children and interact with our lovers and spouses requires us to interface with other "cultures"—people who are different from ourselves. The Fierce Beauties were becoming sufficiently comfortable and rooted in ourselves that we could do this without losing our identity. Our grace, wisdom, love and creativity were just waiting for the right conditions to be released. We were learning how to create those conditions, and as a result, the best of who we were was bursting forth, like seedpods in the wind, to delight and feed the world.

. . .

STEP 8: Learn how to nourish your own soul within your relationships.

CHAPTER 9

Feeding the Spirit

If religion or the sacred is to be discovered or reaffirmed in this culture, it will have to be found under the bed, in a box, like a string of dogwood berries upon which the rosary of life can be sung.
—Lynda Sexson

IT WAS early in December. We had been visited by the first rain of winter, and the newly wet earth breathed a fresh scent of relief. As the women arrived, we prepared Sophie's studio for our meeting, setting up a borrowed slide projector and a screen. In the last couple of months, Sylvia had decisively quit her job and gone off to the Kalahari desert in Africa to spend some time with the San tribe. She had just returned last week and wanted to show us some slides of her trip. The Fierce Beauties had felt her absence during our regular meetings, and we were looking forward to hearing about her adventures with great anticipation.

Sylvia walked through the door with a big grin on her face. Everyone jumped up and clustered around her, talking all at once. She was dressed in a comfortable-looking khaki blouse and pants. Around her neck, she wore several necklaces of small white, brown and black beads, carved, she later told us, from the shells of ostrich eggs. Her hair, which had previously been cut severely short, was beginning to grow out, and curled softly around her ears. On her feet she wore a pair of well-worn, sand-colored leather sandals.

"Wow, Sylvia," exclaimed Allison, "You look so different, you look great!"

"I feel different," Sylvia responded, giving Allison a warm hug.

"I am so glad to be back with all of you, I really missed you," she went on. "In a way, I felt like you were all with me the whole time. I never would have made the journey at all without the support of this group."

Sylvia began to tell us about her trip as she set up her slides and put on a CD of San tribal music. We dimmed the lights and, with the hypnotic sounds of rhythmic clapping and chanting, Sylvia took us into another world. As we encountered images of fierce dark women and men dressed in wild combinations of animal skins and brightly colored cloth, she told us about participating in a tribal ritual dance:

"One night they invited us to be part of a trance dance. Most of the other people on the trek just watched, but I decided to go sit in the circle. The women sat cross-legged on the ground around a fire while the men danced around the outside. The women sang and clapped. In the middle was a trance dancer. Her role was to channel the spirits for the purpose of healing the members of the tribe. The ceremony went on all night, during which time she entered a trance state and went around to various people talking to them and touching them. She came over to me, put her hand on my forehead and looked right at me, or rather, into me.

"The next day I couldn't move. I lay on my bed in my tent weeping. I felt like I'd fallen off the edge of the world. Something in me had cracked open and I was filled with wonder and grief. Looking back on it, it was as if everything that I'd ever believed in and valued had collided abruptly with this magical tribal world. In this alien environment I felt that something larger than myself had recognized and valued me. I felt like I had seen the face of God, and even more importantly, that God had seen me.

"I'm still trying to put myself back together, but I'm definitely not the same person I was before. I feel a part of something. The San believe that they are known by the stars and the sun and the moon. When they die, a star falls to go tell life in another place that something that once stood has now fallen. They know that they are inextricably connected with all life. They have nothing in the way of material wealth, but their spiritual life is very rich.

"I have never thought of myself as a spiritual person," she continued. "But I also had never encountered anything like this. I realized that my concept of religion was that it was something separate from life. To the San, the entire world is imbued with spirit. They don't go to church on Sundays to pray. They live within prayer as they move through life. The world of spirit and the material world aren't divided. It's hard to put into words, but I haven't felt at all lonely since I returned."

Recovering the Indigenous Soul

Those of us who have grown up in highly technological cultures know very little of the worldview of indigenous cultures like the San. In *Of Water and Spirit*, African writer and teacher Malidoma Somé writes, "In the culture of my people, the Dagara, we have no word for the supernatural. The closest we come to this concept is *Yielbongurai*, "the thing that knowledge can't eat." This word suggests that the life and power of certain things depend on their resistance to the kind of categorizing knowledge that human beings apply to everything. In Western reality, there is a clear split between the spiritual and the material, between religious life and secular life. This concept is alien to the Dagara. For us, as in many indigenous cultures, the supernatural is part of our everyday lives."

Describing the life of Australian Aborigines, Nyoongah Mudrooroo writes, "To the Aboriginal person, the entire universe is permeated with life . . . our way of life is spiritual in that there is an interconnectedness, an interrelatedness with all existence, existence extending from the merely physical realms to the spiritual." The spiritual life of indigenous peoples—the indigenous soul—is wedded to the geographical place in which they live. Most indigenous cultures around the world are fighting a losing battle against the loss of their land and their way of life. Yet, for the most part they still retain connections to an ongoing spiritual way of life that many of us presumably "civilized" people have lost.

As we watched Sylvia's slides and talked about her experiences, it provoked a discussion about spirituality and religion.

"This kind of spirituality that Sylvia is talking about is very unfamiliar to me," said Allison. "I've never really been involved with any kind of spiritual practice. We didn't go to church when I grew up. The kinds of rituals and meditations we've done in our group have been the closest I've come to spirituality."

"I went to church all the time when I was a kid," shared Alex, "but it seemed empty and boring to me. I just couldn't relate."

"I know a lot of people who consider themselves spiritual but not religious," Sophie told us. "To them, religion means traditional institutionalized rituals that are empty and without meaning or relevance."

"But don't you think we're missing something?" insisted Sylvia. "Most of us don't have a clue what it is to be deeply connected with spirit in an ongoing way."

"I agree with you Sylvia," said Elinor. "As I've gotten older, my spirituality has become much more important to me. Particularly after my accident and Hugh's death. I needed to make some kind of meaning out of these painful experiences. I think when the fabric of life gets ragged, we have a need to know that there is something more. How else can we survive psychologically in this world? It's frightening to be alive. If we have no spiritual belief, what is the ground that we stand on? Certainly our external reality is constantly changing.

"I needed to believe that there was a sense to it all. Maybe I couldn't be privy to that sensibility, but I needed to have faith that it existed. I've been working on this idea of having faith lately, which is not easy. I aspire to have faith in God. When I can actually experience faith, I relax into my life. I rest easy knowing that whatever happens to me is part of some sacred movement of life. Of course, I fall out of faith all the time. But I work on it. It sounds like the tribal people that Sylvia encountered probably don't struggle with losing their faith."

From the perspective of the indigenous soul, God is immanent—indwelling within all creation. A conversation about the nature of God, or whether or not we believe in God, would be incomprehensible to the San. To them, to be alive is to know God, in the profoundest sense of the word. In *Ordinarily Sacred*, Lynda Sexson writes that, "Religion is not a discrete category within human experience; it is rather a quality that pervades all experience."

My own personal recovery journey, as well as my work with others has taught me that healing psychological wounds cannot be successful without also building an ongoing relationship with a source of spirituality. Being disenfranchised from this connection can cause a myriad of problems including narcissism, depression, loneliness, emptiness and isolation. A therapist friend of mine, Jennifer Freed, believes that, "A spiritual container is essential for women's healing. The suffering that they encounter is more than the small self can contain. We need a larger vessel to hold the parts of us that are mortal in the context of that which is immortal and eternal." It is not important how we create this container, only that we do it.

☀ Fierce Beauty Tip

Spend some time contemplating the condition of your spiritual life. Has your connection to a spiritual source weakened or become stale? It may be time to breathe new life into your existing practice or go in search of a new metaphor. What is your unique style of expressing your spirituality?

Finding Spiritual Meaning in Our Everyday Lives

As contemporary women, to recover our indigenous souls is not an easy task. We have inherited a legacy of spiritual obstacles. Because most of us were raised either without a viable tradition or in a tradition that we experienced as devoid of meaning, our spirituality may be like a hungry ghost wandering without a home. In *Passages of the Soul,* James Roose-Evans writes, "Religion has gone underground and lies buried in the deepest recesses of our psyches, waiting only, like Sleeping Beauty, to be reclaimed."

Most of us do not have deep abiding roots to a particular geographical location that could inform and inspire us. We live in houses that separate us from the natural elemental world. For the most part, our material reality is secure and comfortable, creating the illusion that we do not need to depend on or commune with a spiritual source. We believe that we are in control, rather than being at the mercy of the winds of fate.

The common practices of many institutionalized religions often breed a collective spiritual passivity. We go to a church or a synagogue and expect the priest or rabbi to create the link between the divine and us. Many of us have forgotten how to do it for ourselves. We no longer know how to pray and worship. Creating a spiritual life on our own means taking charge of that connection and discovering our capacity to touch God directly, without intercession. We can either revitalize and deepen into existing traditional rituals or develop our own spiritual metaphors and practices. Mark Gerzon writes, "Whatever our age happens to be when we awaken from our spiritual passivity, it is our spiritual coming of age. We are no longer waiting lazily for the spirit to find us. Nor are we cynically armoring our souls against any experience of the sacred. We are opening our hearts and beginning to seek."

"How do you know God?" I asked the others. "How do you touch the sacred?"

"I feel like my land is a holy place," answered Sophie. "I like this idea of the spirit of place. I'm lucky to live here. It is easy to find God in the beauty here. It makes me happy to have all of you come here to do the kind of deep work that we are doing. I think the spirits of this land have been blessing us."

"My grandma always used to say that God was in the quiet places," said Lena, thoughtfully. "There are times very early in the morning when I go sit out in my garden and listen to the day wake up. It's quiet and fresh. I feel a sweetness that fills me with gratitude for being alive. I try to remember to do it regularly. It's so easy to dwell on the things that don't work. But I've also felt the presence of something sacred in the midst of listening to great music. Eduardo and I were down at a café by the ocean the other day where there was a band playing wonderful Brazilian jazz. The weather was warm, the water sparkled and there was a contagious joyous spirit in the air. It felt like a holy moment."

"I had a realization recently," shared Jenny, "that God was in the hard places. This year has been so difficult that there were times that I felt abandoned by anything sacred. But out of sheer desperation I discovered that I could reach out toward a deeper presence. I found that when I did that, something actually happened. I had moments when I could feel that something larger than me loved and valued me."

"I think that God is in depth," offered Elinor, "any kind of depth. It's so easy to move through life just touching the surfaces of people and situations. When I take the time to deepen into a particular moment or person, there is a different quality of energy that is present. I think you can find God anywhere, but it takes a certain kind of attention, a focus on depth. It's a perception that makes a moment sacred."

Different Ways to Touch the Sacred

There are many ways to experience a sacred presence or connection in the course of our everyday lives. We do not need to wait for a church service or another person to make it happen. Participating in a community of people who share ritual space can be a wonderfully fulfilling experience, providing us with support, company and shared celebration. If we lack that community, however, it is still important to find ways to create a spiritual practice on our own. For some, quiet meditation or prayer is the vehicle. Others worship through celebratory song and dance.

An ongoing connection with our spirituality can be enhanced through deepening our appreciation for things that we may take for granted in our ordinary lives. A poet friend, Carla Martinez, writes of being moved by the beauty of her land:

> *In the wilderness where I live*
> *Wandering among the constellations*
> *Of precious brilliance*
> *Your presence blesses me*
> *And whispers poetry*
> *Into the bodies of canyons.*

Noticing the beauty of our world is a way of reorganizing and retraining ourselves to place a greater emphasis on the positive. The concept of sin in the Christian faith speaks more to a state of negativity, fear and insufficiency than to moral deficiency—a loss of grace. Nora Gallagher in *Things Seen and Unseen* asserts that, "The opposite of sin is not virtue but faith." Having faith means being able to trust at the most fundamental level of our being. It means believing in our bones that the world is a benevolent place and that the god of our imagination is a benevolent god. It is a difficult state for many of us to achieve with any consistency and also potentially very rewarding. When we live in faith, we can journey through life with grace. The hard edges soften as we move fluidly and easily through the complex challenges that come our way.

One way of connecting with the sacred is through the act of prayer, which we also can imagine as a way of focusing or "being with" ourselves in a deeper way. Prayer is a vehicle for tending the soul that is personal and immediate. Auguste Sabatier, a nineteenth-century French theologian, says that prayer is "no vain exercise of words, no mere representation of sacred formulae, but the very movement of the soul itself, putting itself in a personal relation of contact with the mysterious power of which it feels the presence—it may be even before it has a name to call it. Whenever this interior prayer is lacking, there is no religion; wherever, on the other hand, this prayer rises and stirs the soul, even in the absence of forms or doctrines, we have living religion."

☀Fierce Beauty Tip

If you are not familiar with praying, it can be a good thing to try. Find a private place and imagine that you are in conversation with your God. Speaking out loud, tell this sacred presence everything on your mind. Speak until you are empty and there is nothing more to be said. Notice how this feels in your body and heart.

The Art of Creative Ritual

Another way to sustain the thread of spiritual connection as we move through life is to create rituals to honor significant occasions. In general, our culture lacks sacred rituals that mark transitions and celebrate key events. We have many common secular rituals like watching the Super Bowl, receiving diplomas or giving someone a watch upon retirement, but we lack rituals that genuinely take us into depth, feeling and an appreciation of the divine.

An active ceremonial life in a community can tend the soul of both the individuals and the group as a whole. I recently helped a young woman design a ceremony to mark the completion of her master's thesis. She felt that she was ready to fully enter into life as an adult. She wanted to invite her family, friends and key helpers along the way to witness and celebrate this moment.

She and I designed a very simple ceremony. We assembled in a circle in a special place that she had chosen out in nature. We sat around an altar that she had created that included items like her thesis, pictures of her loved ones and her master's degree. One by one each person gave her small gifts and shared the ways in which they recognized and honored who she was and her accomplishments. The ceremony created a vehicle for people to speak their truth and share their love. She even received blessings from members of her family who had previously been estranged. Not only was she deeply moved by what was said, but also the whole group felt blessed to have participated.

Although some people feel initially awkward at events like this one, because they seem unfamiliar, they get over that discomfort rapidly and are extremely gratified to have an opportunity for depth and authenticity. We hunger to go below the surface, to go below contrived social occasions that are filled with empty platitudes. In *Earth Angels: Engaging the*

Sacred in Everyday Things, Shaun McNiff proclaims that, "True ritual should indeed *set fire* to us all . . . we long to speak heart to heart, to be set fire to, to come alive, to live authentically."

Ritual opportunities abound in the course of our lives. In our time together, the Fierce Beauty Club had used them for personal healing, as well as to access our creativity, deepen our sexuality, get rid of unwanted psychological baggage and tend our relationships. Learning to create meaningful ceremonies of one's own design is an important step in becoming empowered as the agent of your own spirituality. Not only can we develop new ways of celebrating events like birthdays, retirements and graduations, we can also bring fresh energy into established rituals that may have grown stale or outdated.

Rituals take us beneath the ordinary, surface nature of existence. They are also quite simple to design. The first step of ritual creation is to clarify your intention. We may, for example, want to bless a house that we are moving into. Our intention is to inhabit a home that is safe, happy, nurturing and free of stress. We want to get rid of any undesirable energy and then welcome in sweet energy. The actual actions, words or objects used in any given ceremony are symbolic by nature and completely individual in taste. We could symbolically clean a house by sprinkling fresh, purified water. We can burn incense or herbs like sage to make the air sweet. We could also walk the perimeter of the house ringing a bell or beating a drum. In truth, it doesn't matter exactly what is done, but that we take the time, energy and focus to tend the spiritual dimension of life.

Many spiritual traditions believe that we need to feed the spirits if they are to feed us in return. Creative ritual is a way of feeding the spirits. Rituals are like opening doorways between the physical world and the world of spirit. In *The Joy of Ritual*, Barbara Biziou explains that, "We literally join the metaphysical with the physical as a means of calling spirit into our material lives...thus we are able to bring a sacred feeling to everyday events, transforming them into times of quiet reflection and connection."

Rituals provide opportunities for the expression of deep feelings. Many years ago, I had the very difficult and painful experience of getting pregnant just as I was ending my marriage to my ex-husband. I had two dependent children and limited financial and emotional resources. After much soul searching, I chose to have an abortion. I gathered my family and friends together and we all said prayers and blessings for this being. Feeling intuitively that she was a girl, I named her Joy. I made a small velvet bag for her in which we placed small gifts. In the ceremony I was able to express the love that I felt for her during the short period that she was with me and my grief about letting her go. I went later and cast the small bag into the ocean. I know other women who, with a similar intention, have planted trees in honor of their unborn children.

We can create rituals to mark our beginnings and our endings. Some years ago at a holiday family gathering, I invited my sisters to join me in a ritual to mourn and symbolically let go of our mother. Although she had died long ago when we were still children, I felt that her spirit was still bound to each one of us in a painful and unhealthy way. We talked about her, I read a poem and then we lifted our arms and imagined releasing her spirit so that we could all move on.

There are four basic steps to the art of creative ritual:

1. Decide what your intention or purpose is and whether this is an individual or group ritual.

2. Create sacred space through the use of prayer and breathing exercises, lighting candles, using scents or incense, sounds or movements and using symbolic ritual objects.

3. Signify a clear beginning and end to this period of sacred space.

4. Once you have created a ritual container, allow yourself and others, if present, to access and express deep feelings, inner truth and wisdom.

Welcoming Our Young Women

In the lives of women there are two transitions that are particularly important to mark in a ceremonial manner: the time when a young girl comes of age as a woman and then again when she moves out of childbearing years into elderhood. If we neglect to find ways to tend the feminine soul through thoughtful ceremony at these junctures, it is difficult, as Mary Oliver writes, to find our "place in the family of things." We don't know our value, the gifts that we have to give our families and communities and our place in a lineage of women. Ceremonies bestow not only spiritual power but a sense of membership in the larger community.

When a young girl begins to menstruate and her body takes on the form of a mature woman, she enters into a mystery that involves sexuality, power, seduction, procreation, and motherhood. She enters the complex world of the feminine that is, for the most part, little understood. There are a number of ways that she can get confused or even lost. Many young girls enter adulthood, as we've discussed earlier, with inadequate role models and guides into the mysteries of womanhood. As a result, as Mary Pipher described so well in *Reviving Ophelia*, we see the casualties all around us of young women who starve themselves to death, are consumed with self-hatred or are mired in addictive behaviors.

Eating disorders in young women are diseases of the feminine soul. They reflect a self-hatred of the feminine body that by no means begins with the young women who manifest symptoms. These young women are overtly displaying the effects of an inherited loss of self-love and respect that has affected multiple generations of women before them. The antidote to this disease is, first, for adult women, like the members of the Fierce Beauty Club, to find ways to tend our own wounds and reclaim our power. Then, second, we can reach out to the generation who follows and extend our welcome, our wisdom and our willingness to help them understand and love their womanhood. We can create rites of passage for young women that include them in a web of female connection that will sustain and inform them as they negotiate their way through life.

"I would love it if you all could help me create a rite of passage for my 15-year-old daughter, Diana," requested Jenny, as we chatted about the need for initiations. "I've been telling her about the Fierce Beauty Club and she's kind of intrigued. She's already gotten her period, but I'd still like to do something to recognize that she's becoming a woman."

"Why don't you bring her to one of our meetings?" suggested Elinor. "She could get to know us."

"That would be good but I've also been thinking about inviting some of her friends and doing a group for teenage girls," answered Jenny. "I think she would enjoy it more if she had her friends with her. I want to meet with some of the other parents and design a relevant, meaningful experience for the girls."

When my daughter, Noelani, was about 13 years old, Aaron and I invited her to participate in a coming of age ceremony. First we asked her to build an altar that was a visual representation of her feminine soul. Then, several of my women friends and I took her out into the forest. We blindfolded her and walked her through the woods to a spot by a small river.

There we took off her blindfold and sat down together on rocks by the side of the river. My friend Sara produced a pot of tea, teacups and cookies. Noelani was then given the opportunity to access the wisdom and experience of the elder women. She asked her "aunties" many tough questions about sexuality, menstruation, men, pregnancy, aging and beauty issues. When she felt finished, we ritually bathed her in the cool, clear river water and then dressed her in a new white dress. After that we returned to our house, where the men were waiting. Sitting in a circle around her altar, we presented her to the men who warmly welcomed her as a woman.

There are many ways to design contemporary rites of passage for young women. The most important elements usually include: 1) some form of ritualized separation from the child part of the psyche, 2) an opportunity for instruction by her elders and 3) a recognition and celebration of the fledgling woman. Some ceremonies, in the tradition of Native American vision quests, involve a period of time spent alone. In traditional cultures the young initiates often live separately from the tribe while they undergo various challenges and rigors. In our culture, there is little support for such extensive rituals, but we can still find ways to bring meaning, depth and honor to this crucial time in young women's spiritual and psychological development. If it is not possible to create a formal rite of passage, it is also of great value for older women to take the time to forge mentoring relationships with younger women.

☀Fierce Beauty Tip

Find a young woman in your community who could use some adult female mentorship and offer your services. This can be done formally through a mentoring organization or informally with a friend's child. Spend quality time with this young woman. Share your own experience and wisdom. Let her know that you honor and respect who she is.

Blessing Our Elders

The other crossroad in women's lives that needs to be specially honored is the point when we move beyond menopause into elderhood. In our culture, this phase of life represents an entry into obscurity for most women. We fail to value the resources of older people, particularly women, and often ignore their capacity to act as spiritual and moral leaders for our communities. In other societies around the world, older women are revered because their closer proximity to the spirit world gives them access to spiritual power. In *Force of Character*, James Hillman describes this time of life as one in which, "One's primary ground of being has moved to the soul," and states that elders are "halfway to the ghost status of the ancestors and to the naked sensitivity of pure spirits."

In Malidoma Somé's Dagara tradition, the elders are the temporal voices of the wisdom of the ancestors. They have an essential role in tempering and guiding the lives of younger members of the tribe. In *Reclaimed Powers*, David Guttman says that older women in indigenous cultures become, "more powerful in the religious rituals of their people. . . . At the same time that she is gaining secular power in ritual, family affairs, and community politics, the older woman may also be gaining supernatural power." For most aging women in our culture, this vision of elderhood is a far cry from the reality they face. We can, however, remedy this predicament through creating ceremonies that install women in their rightful office as transmitters of wisdom.

Recently, some women have been having "croning" ceremonies, often at 50th birthdays. These ceremonies seek to empower women in their aging process. I participated in one celebration in which all the participants gathered in a circle, with those over 50 on one side and those under 50 on the other. The birthday woman was instructed to sit on the under-50 side, which was marked by a line of glitter going down the middle of the circle. The ceremony began with the elders on the over-50 side giving her their advice about the aging process. After that, two of the older women escorted her to the center of the circle and gave her a bowl of water to symbolically wash off anything that she did not want to bring with her into this new phase of life. After this ritual cleansing, she was wrapped in a ceremonial robe and led across the threshold to the elder side of the circle. She was then invited to step into the role of the Crone by sharing her wisdom with the group.

"In some of the women's classes that I host," I told the group, "I invite the older postmenopausal women to sit on one side of the room together and give a teaching to the rest of the women. Why don't we do that here tonight?"

We all looked expectantly at Elinor. She looked hesitantly at Lena. "Are you with me?"

"Sure, it's been two years now since I had a period." Lena responded, with a hoot. "I guess I qualify as an elder of sorts."

She went over and sat down next to Elinor on the couch. The rest of us rearranged ourselves in a semicircle facing them.

"It's strange to be sitting here," said Elinor. "In my insides, I don't feel old at all. I get surprised at the face that I see when I look in the mirror. But through the time we've spent together in the Fierce Beauty Club, I've come to appreciate these lines on my face. I think that learning to love the soul that's etched into my face is the greatest gift that I can give to younger women. I like to recite this poem to myself that was written by Joseph Campbell. It says:

> As a burning candle
> In a holy place
> So is the beauty
> Of an aging face.

"I want to tell all of you that there's nothing to fear about getting old. Not if we have each other." There were tears shining brightly in her eyes as she looked at all of us. "The older I get the closer I feel to my feminine soul. I can feel this deep river flowing out of me. And when I look at each of you, I see so much beauty and strength. I think we are each candles burning in a holy place."

Lena was solemn as she spoke: "I think the greatest gift I could give to all of you is to truly see you. When I think back to when we first started meeting together, we were so different. It's like we were just shades of what we are now. It's as if each one of us has emerged out of hiding. Now we're really here. To me, getting older is about getting more here with every year. And I can see that happening to us."

She continued, turning to face each of us directly as she spoke: "Sylvia went on the greatest adventure of her life and came back a whole new person. Jenny's life fell apart and she turned into a butterfly. Allison transformed from a hesitant girl into a confident woman. Alex relaxed for the first time in her life. Sophie leapt into the great unknown with her art and is still here to tell the tale. I've met the man of my dreams and haven't turned into a puddle of mush, and Elinor is a shining example to us all of a juicy, vital old lady. And through all of this our group has been the thread that has connected each one of us pearls. I am very grateful for what we've shared together."

☀️Fierce Beauty Tip

Reach out to an older woman in your family or community. Ask her to tell you stories of her life. How are the ancestors speaking through her? Give her the gift of honoring her life experience and listen carefully for the gift she gives you.

Deepening into Each Moment

Tending the sacred as we move through our lives is a process of learning to savor deeply each of the experiences served up to us on the platter of life. In the Buddhist tradition, this is called mindfulness. Practitioners cultivate mindfulness by disciplining themselves to slow down and breathe at periodic intervals during the day. In this way they can feel, taste, see and hear what life offers in a more aware manner.

It is all too easy to consume life rapidly without fully digesting and appreciating its profound richness. Prayer, meditations and rituals of all varieties help us to be more fully present in each moment. Regardless of the particular practice, developing mindfulness helps us honor the beauty and meaning that imbues our world. Through our attention, we are healed. As we go beneath the surface of things and honor the wondrous and complex rhythms of life, we join and are joined in that vibrant dance—eating the food, drinking the wine, wailing with grief and laughing with ecstatic joy. In this way we say "yes!" to the great round of birthing and dying, beginning and ending, that cycles in and out, within us and around us.

. . .

STEP 9: Tend the sacred as you move through your life passages.

Conclusion

THE PROCESS of living is a process of being born over and over again. The Fierce Beauty Club had, in many ways, been the midwife for that birthing process in each one of us. The container of the group tended each one of us as we moved from seedling to full flower. It created safety, a place to see deeply into ourselves and consistent opportunities to be seen and mirrored by others. The group was confrontational at times, unwilling to allow any one of us to stay stuck in unhealthy habits of victimization and self-neglect. Not only did we pool the resources that existed in the rich life experience of the Fierce Beauties, we also cast our net widely into the world to catch anything that would help us to know more about who we were.

One of the most significant aspects of our healing process was to place ourselves within a historical legacy of strong, fierce, beautiful women—the Motherline. We worked first toward reweaving the broken threads with our own mothers, and then, reaching back into history, we explored our connections with feminine archetypes throughout time. Inspired by the richness and diversity of feminine expression, we knew, without a doubt, that we were powerful and that we could be anything that we wanted to be.

At times, the group became a sacred place that hosted parts of us within its fierce boundary that we could barely feel much less claim in our daily lives. Within that protected circle, we were able to retrieve and hold onto a different concept of beauty that was evoked through connection with our souls and our sensual bodies. And in that sacred container, we could delve into the largely undiscovered mystery of feminine sexuality. Over and over again, the Fierce Beauty Club discovered that the way to power, beauty, sexuality, creativity, emotional sustenance and wholeness came through connecting with a spiritual source that woke us up, fed us, vitalized us and brought us to a place inside ourselves that was home.

Not only did we become artists of our own personal transformation, each Fierce Beauty made a strong commitment to her creative life. Dedicating ourselves to our deep creativity filled us with purpose and passion. We saw that we each had something of value to offer and bless our community. We were inspired to bring those gifts back to our families and workplaces, knowing that the world needs desperately what we have to give.

We decided that there were certain key qualities that we aspired to embrace and embody in our lives. We defined a Fierce Beauty as:

- A woman who refuses victim status and takes full responsibility for her own destiny
- A woman in communion with the deep river of her feminine soul
- A woman not ruled by anyone's fantasies but her own
- A woman who embraces her desire for relationships, as well as her craving for aloneness, independence and creativity
- A woman who knows that she is beautiful in her own unique way and worthy of love and respect for who she is instead of how she looks
- A woman who celebrates her female body through all its changing faces and phases of life
- A woman who unabashedly expresses her distinctive style of female sensuality

- A woman who has found her personal vision to contribute to the world
- A woman who can serve herself without abandoning her children, family and community
- A woman who is so full of herself that her cup runneth over and blesses the world

The Fierce Beauty Club still continues to meet. Some members have moved on and new ones have joined. Some women went on to start their own spin-off groups. Regardless of the form, however, each one of us has found ways to create and sustain some form of women's community in our lives. We learned through our experience together that this kind of quality contact with other women is essential to our continued growth and well-being.

As women, it is all too easy in this world to forget who we are. There are powerful forces that distract and divert us away from the power and the beauty of the feminine soul. A deluge of soulless images of youth-obsessed women rain down upon us, and it is easy to drown. The pace of our culture continues to move ever faster, driving us collectively into superficiality and spiritual hunger. When we try to maintain our sense of ourselves without the help of "sister mirrors," we often find ourselves slipping back into old self-annihilating patterns. We can get lost in the conflicting demands and pressures of the people around us. When Fierce Beauties find and reach out to one another, however, we create an oasis, a homecoming.

So, whoever and wherever you are, there is some other woman who will understand. If you have lost the thread of your feminine soul, together you can help each other reconnect the strands and create a tapestry of your life that wraps around you like a soft warm blanket. We were never meant to make this journey alone. Together we can take heart, awaken the deep song, fan the fires of fierce femininity and find a place of grace.

In fierce beauty it is done.

Fierce Beauty Steps

1. Create regular ongoing connection with your women friends.

2. Assert your unique style of fierce feminine power.

3. Embrace the Divine Feminine within you.

4. Reclaim the lost and forgotten parts of your psyche.

5. Connect with your soul beauty and sensuality.

6. Awaken and celebrate your sacred sexuality.

7. Discover and express your creative passion.

8. Learn how to nourish your soul within your relationships.

9. Tend the sacred as you move through your life passages.

Endnotes

INTRODUCTION

xvi   Katie Roiphe, *Last Night in Paradise: Sex and Morals at the Century's End* (Boston: Little, Brown and Co., 1997), p. 193.

xv   Karen Lehrman, *The Lipstick Proviso: Women, Sex and Power in the Real World* (New York: Anchor Books, 1997), pp. 36, 42.

CHAPTER 1

1   Geneen Roth, *Appetites: On the Search for True Nourishment,* (New York: Dutton, 1996), p. 140.

7   Helen Fisher, *The First Sex: The Natural Talents of Women and How They Are Changing the World* (New York: Random House, 1999), p. 40.

10   Joan Borysenko, Ph.D., *Woman's Book of Life: Biology, Psychology, Spirituality of the Feminine Life Cycle* (New York: Riverhead Books, 1996), p. 88.

10   *Ibid.,* p. 5.

13   Danielle Crittenden, *What Our Mothers Didn't Tell Us: Why Happiness Eludes the Modern Woman* (New York: Simon & Schuster, 1999), pp. 21–22.

15   Roth, *op. cit.,* p. 149.

18   Louise Carus Mahdi, Steven Foster and Meredith Little, *Betwixt and Between: Patterns of Masculine and Feminine Initiation* (La Salle, Ill.: Open Court, 1987), p. 241.

CHAPTER 2

22   Nelson Mandela, Inaugural Speech, 1994.

24   Rollo May, *Power and Innocence* (New York: W. W. Norton and Co., 1972), p. 48.

24   Naomi Wolf, *Fire with Fire* (New York: Random House, 1993), pp. 135, 144.

28 Marianne Williamson, *Women's Worth* (New York: Random House, 1993), p. 9.

28 Harriet Rubin, *The Princessa: Machiavelli for Women* (New York: Currency Books, 1997), p. 8.

28 Fisher, *op. cit.*, pp. 154, 170.

31 Fisher, *op. cit.*, p. 29.

32 Aaron Kipnis, *Knights Without Armor* (Los Angeles: Jeremy P. Tarcher Inc., 1991), p. 49.

33 Williamson, *op. cit.*, p. 105.

34 Kipnis, *op. cit.*, p. 24.

34 Deborah Tannen, *You Just Don't Understand* (New York: William Morrow and Co., 1990), p. 76.

34 Fisher, *op. cit.*, pp. 61–62.

35 Mary Batten, *Sexual Strategies: How Females Choose Their Mates* (New York: Jeremy P. Tarcher/Putnam, 1992), p. 63.

37 Geraldine Brooks, *Nine Parts of Desire: The Hidden World of Islamic Women* (New York: Anchor Books, 1995).

37 Barbara Walker, *The Woman's Encyclopedia of Myths and Secrets* (New York: Harper & Row, 1983), p. 217.

38 *Ibid.*, p. 832.

38 Rachel Misdrahe-Capon, *Sanctuaries and Museums in Greece: Delphi* (Athens, Greece: Orpheus Editions, 1976), p. 7.

39 May, *op. cit.*, p. 19.

40 Warren Farrell, *Why Men Are the Way They Are* (New York: McGraw-Hill, 1986), p. 10.

46 Rubin, *op. cit.*, p. 62

46 Anne Cameron, *Daughters of Copper Woman* (Vancouver, BC: Press Gang Publishers, 1981), p. 134.

CHAPTER 3

48 Charlene Spretnek, *Lost Goddesses of Early Greece* (Boston: Beacon Press, 1984), p. 72.

50 Rosemary Radford Ruether, *Gaia and God: An Ecofeminist Theology of Earth Healing* (San Francisco: HarperSanFrancisco, 1992), p. 166.

61 Diane Wolkstein and Samuel Noah Kramer, *Inanna, Queen of Heaven and Earth* (New York: Harper & Row, 1983), p. 17.

62 Walker, *op. cit.*, 1983, p. 453.

62 Caitlin Matthews, *Sophia, Goddess of Wisdom* (London: Mandala Books, 1991), p. 66.

63 Mary Oliver, *Dream Work* (New York: Atlantic Monthly Press, 1986), p. 14.

63 Clarissa Pinkola Estés, *Women Who Run With the Wolves* (New York: Ballantine Books, 1992, 1995), p. 10.

64 Herb Kawainui Kane, *Pele: Goddess of Hawaii's Volcanoes* (Captain Cook, Hawaii: The Kawainui Press, 1987), p. 23.

64 Estés, *op. cit.*, p. 28.

66 Christine Downing, *The Goddess: Mythological Images of the Feminine* (New York: Crossroads Publishing Co., 1987), p. 195.

66 Felix Guirand, ed., *New Larousse Encyclopedia of Mythology* (New York: Crescent Books, 1989), p. 437. Also Barbara Walker, p. 172, 1094.

66 Maya Deren, *The Divine Horseman* (New York: Delta, 1970), p. 141

68 George Hart, *A Dictionary of Egyptian Gods and Goddesses* (London: Routledge & Kegan Paul, 1986), p. 188.

68 Manfred Lurker, *The Gods and Symbols of Ancient Egypt* (London: Thames and Hudson Ltd., 1980), p. 106.

69 Kane, *op. cit.*, pp. 5–7.

69 Luisah Teish, *Jambalaya* (San Francisco: HarperSanFrancisco, 1985), p. 120.

70 Walker, *op. cit.*, 1983, p. 172, and Guirand, pp. 431–36.

70 Walker, *op. cit.*, 1983, p. 518.

71 Barbara Walker, *The Crone: Women of Age, Wisdom and Power* (San Francisco: HarperSanFrancisco, 1985), p. 48.

73 *Ibid.*, p. 52.

73 *Ibid.*, p. 50.

73 Sheila Moon, *Changing Woman and Her Sisters* (San Francisco: Guild for Psychological Studies Publishing House, 1984), p. 145.

73 *Ibid.*, p. 138.

74 Matthews, *op. cit.*, p. 119.

CHAPTER 4

78 Connie Zweig, Ph.D., and Steve Wolf, Ph.D, *Romancing the Shadow* (New York: Ballantine, 1997), p. 6

79 Esther Harding, *Woman's Mysteries: Ancient and Modern* (New York: Putnam, for the C. G. Jung Foundation for Analytical Psychology, 1972), p. 79.

80 Maren Tonder Hansen, *Mother Mysteries* (Boston: Shambala Publications Inc., 1997), p. 29.

80 Borysenko, *op. cit.*, p. 165.

83 Mahdi, Foster, Little, *op. cit.*, p. 279.

84 Wolkstein and Kramer, *op. cit.*, p. 52.

85 Wolkstein and Kramer. *op. cit.*, p. 60.

86 Jane Wagner, *The Search for Signs of Intelligent Life in the Universe* (New York: Harper & Row, 1986), p. 15.

95 Linda Schierse Leonard, *Meeting the Madwoman: An Inner Challenge for Feminine Spirit* (New York: Bantam Books, 1993), p. 4.

96 Natalie Angier, *Woman: An Intimate Geography* (New York: Houghton Mifflin Co., 1999), p. 235.

96 Elizabeth Debold, Marie Wilson and Idelisse Malave, *Mother Daughter Revolution: From Betrayal to Power* (Reading, Mass.: Addison-Wesley Publishing Co., 1993), p. xvi.

99 Paula Caplan, *Don't Blame Mother: Mending the Mother-Daughter Relationship* (New York: Harper & Row, 1989), p. 151.

CHAPTER 5

103 Estés, *op. cit.*, p. 202.

104 Naomi Wolf, *The Beauty Myth* (New York: William Morrow, 1991), p. 185.

104 *Ibid.*, p. 184.

104 Women's Action Coalition, *WAC Stats: The Facts About Women* (New York: The New Press, 1993), p. 20.

105 As seen on *Secrets of Beauty Pageants,* shown on UPN network, 5/11/98.

105 Halcomb B. Noble, "Steroid use by teenage girls is rising," *Santa Barbara News Press,* June 6, 1999, p. D1.

107 Elisabeth Rosenthal, "Women Have the Wrong Idea About Breast Size," *New York Times,* July 27, 1992, pp. D1-4.

110 James Hillman, *Thought of the Heart, Eranos Lectures No. 2* (Dallas: Spring Publications, 1981), p. 29.

110 Thomas Moore, *The Soul of Sex* (New York: HarperCollins, 1998), p. 32.

110 Christine Downing, *The Goddess: Mythological Images of the Feminine* (New York: The Crossroad Publishing Co., 1987), p. 195.

114 Wolf, *op. cit.*, p 182. Also Joan Crowder, "Epidemic on Display," *Santa Barbara News Press,* May 12, 1998, p. D1. Also Joan Jacobs Brumberg, *Fasting Girls: The Emergence of Anorexia as a Modern Disease* (Cambridge, Mass.: Harvard University Press, 1988), p. 20.

115 Rita Freedman, *Beauty Bound* (Lexington, Mass.: D. C. Heath and Co., 1986), p. 160.

117 Nancy Friday, *The Power of Beauty* (New York: HarperCollins, 1986), p. 33.

CHAPTER 6

129 Olivia St. Claire, *Unleashing the Sex Goddess in Every Woman* (New York: Harmony Books, 1996), p. 23.

133 Associated Press, "Survey: Sexual Dysfunction Common," *USA Today,* 2/10/99. Nicholas-Hays, Inc., 1997, p. 19.

137 Dr. Christiane Northrup, M.D., *Women's Bodies, Women's Wisdom* (New York: Bantam, 1994), p. 232.

139 Sally Wendkos Olds, *The Eternal Garden: Seasons of our Sexuality* (New York: Times Books, 1985), p. 30.

139 *Ibid.,* p. 33.

139 Fisher, *op. cit.,* p. 202.

139 Northrup, *op. cit.,* p. 225.

139 Sarah Blaffer Hrdy, *The Woman That Never Evolved* (Cambridge, Mass.: Harvard University Press, 1981), p. 176.

140 Olds, *op. cit.,* p. 90.

140 Angier, *op. cit.,* p. 72.

141 Dalma Heyn, *The Erotic Silence of the American Wife* (New York: Turtle Bay Books, 1992), p. 70.

143 St. Claire, *op. cit.,* p. 49.

143 David Steinberg, ed., *The Erotic Impulse* (New York: Jeremy P. Tarcher/Perigee Books, 1992), p. 123.

146 Moore, *op. cit.,* p. 13.

CHAPTER 7

152 Thomas Moore, *Care of the Soul* (New York: HarperCollins, 1992), p. 199.

155 Estés, *op. cit.,* p. 299.

156 Federico Garcia Lorca, *In Search of Duende* (New York: New Directions Bibelot, 1998), p. 49.

158 James Hillman, *The Soul's Code* (New York: Random House, 1996), p. 1.

161 Linda Firestone, *Awakening Minerva: The Power of Creativity in Women's Lives* (New York: Warner Books, 1997), p. 57.

175 Williamson, *op. cit.,* p. 12.

CHAPTER 8

177 Stephen Levine, *Who Dies?* (New York: Anchor Books, 1982), p. 87.

178 Heyn, 1997, *op. cit.*, p. xii.

182 Borysenko, *op. cit.*, p. 102.

183 John Gray, Ph.D., *Men Are from Mars, Women Are from Venus* (New York: HarperCollins, 1992), p. 31.

183 Erich Neumann, *Amor and Psyche: the Psychic Development of the Feminine* (New York: Bollingen Series LIV, Princeton University Press, 1956), p. 27.

183 *Ibid.*, p. 85.

184 Guirand, *op. cit.*, p. 378.

186 John Welwood, Ph.D., *Journey of the Heart* (New York: Harper-Perennial, 1990), p. 22.

196 *Ibid.*, p. 8.

196 *Ibid.*, p. 47.

196 Zweig and Wolf, *op. cit.*, p. 146.

197 Robert Bly, "A Man and a Woman" from *Selected Poems of Robert Bly* (New York: HarperCollins, 1986).

CHAPTER 9

201 Lynda Sexson, *Ordinarily Sacred* (Charlottesville The University Press of Virginia, 1992), p. 7.

203 Laurens van der Post and Jean-Marc Pottiez, *A Walk with a White Bushman* (New York: William Morrow and Co., 1986), p. 31.

203 Malidoma Somé, *Of Water and Spirit* (New York: Jeremy P. Tarcher/Putnam, 1994), p. 8.

203 Nyoongah Mudrooroo, *Aboriginal Mythology* (London: Aquarian, 1994), p. vii.

205 Sexson, *op. cit.*, p. 7.

206 James Roose-Evans, *Passages of the Soul* (Shaftesbury, Dorset: Element Books, 1994), p. 2.

206 Mark Gerzon, *Coming Into Our Own* (New York: Delacorte Press, 1992), p. 258.

208 Carla Martinez, John Souza and Toni Wynn, *Colors, Voices, Place* (Santa Barbara, Calif.: Mille Grazie Press & SeaMoon Press, 1997), p. 29.

209 Nora Gallagher, *Things Seen and Unseen: A Year Lived in Faith* (New York: Alfred A. Knopf, 1998), p. 78.

209 William James, *Varieties of Religious Experience* (New York: The Modern Library, 1936), p. 454.

211 Shaun McNiff, *Earth Angels: Engaging the Sacred in Everyday Things* (Boston & London: Shambala Publications Inc., 1995), p. 53.

212 Barbara Biziou, *The Joy of Ritual* (New York: Golden Books, 1999), pp. 10–11.

213 *Ibid.*, pp. 14–15

213 Mary Oliver, *Dream Work* (New York: Atlantic Monthly Press, 1986), p. 14.

214 Mary Pipher, *Reviving Ophelia* (New York: Putnum, 1994).

216 James Hillman, *Force of Character and the Lasting Life* (New York: Random House, 1999), pp. xxiv, xvi.

216 David Guttman, *Reclaimed Powers: Toward a New Psychology of Men and Women in Later Life* (New York: Basic Books, Inc., 1987), p. 182.

217 Helen Bransford, *Welcome to Your Facelift* (New York: Doubleday, 1997), p. 151.